D0301301

Comedy, Cameos, and Campaign Communication

Leveraging Entertainment Media to
Win Elections and Advance Policy

Jason Turcotte

Routledge
Taylor & Francis Group

NEW YORK AND LONDON

First published 2024
by Routledge
605 Third Avenue, New York, NY 10158

and by Routledge
4 Park Square, Milton Park, Abingdon, Oxon, OX14 4RN

Routledge is an imprint of the Taylor & Francis Group, an informa business

Library of Congress Cataloging-in-Publication Data
Names: Turcotte, Jason, author.
Title: Comedy, cameos, and campaign communication : leveraging
   entertainment media to win elections and advance policy / Jason Turcotte.
Description: First edition. | New York : Routledge, 2024. | Series: Routledge
   studies in media, communication, and politics | Includes bibliographical
   references and index.
Identifiers: LCCN 2023036643 (print) | LCCN 2023036644 (ebook) |
   ISBN 9781032429076 (pbk) | ISBN 9781032429052 (hbk) |
   ISBN 9781003364832 (ebk)
Subjects: LCSH: Political campaigns. | Communication in politics. |
   Mass media—Political aspects. | Television broadcasting of news. |
   Television programs—Political aspects. | Political participation.
Classification: LCC JF1001 .T865 20247 (print) | LCC JF1001 (ebook) |
   DDC 320.1/4—dc23/eng/20230912
LC record available at https://lccn.loc.gov/2023036643
LC ebook record available at https://lccn.loc.gov/2023036644

ISBN: 978-1-032-42905-2 (hbk)
ISBN: 978-1-032-42907-6 (pbk)
ISBN: 978-1-003-36483-2 (ebk)

DOI: 10.4324/9781003364832

Typeset in Times New Roman
by Apex CoVantage, LLC

Contents

Acknowledgments

I have many people to thank for inspiring this text and motivating me to forge ahead with the project. I owe tremendous gratitude to my supportive colleagues in the Communication Department at Cal Poly Pomona and the many intellectually curious students I've had in my political communication courses over the years. A great deal of thanks goes to student research assistant (and now journalist) Janean Sorrell. This project would not have been possible without her assistance and enthusiasm. Much gratitude to my dissertation chair Kirby Goidel for guidance in navigating the process, illustrator Eduardo Rangel for helping to bring case studies to life, and my family, friends, and partner Chris for their confidence in me. Finally, many thanks to publisher Felisa Salvago-Keyes who saw merit in this project early on and helped see this text come to fruition.

1 The long tail

The effects of media choice and audience fragmentation on the campaign process

Do you remember a time when you encountered one of your professors or grade-school teachers out doing something fun? A rock or rap concert, perhaps, a Marvel movie premiere or a night out at a favorite watering hole. You probably processed the encounter with some degree of intrigue or confusion, silently examining your teacher as if they were an animal that broke free from the local zoo. You probably thought, "What are *they* doing *here*?"

It wasn't all that long ago when voters might have had that same reaction to a presidential candidate appearing on *Saturday Night Live* or a popular sitcom. "What were *they* doing *here*?" they might ask. For decades, the domain of political campaigns was largely confined to news and information media. These are the media where campaigns and political elites would choose to connect with voters and constituents through. Candidates 50 years ago may make a Sunday morning appearance on the rigid *Meet the Press* on NBC. They might sit down for a profile interview published in *The New York Times* or pen an op-ed in *The Wall Street Journal*. But you wouldn't catch them revealing personal stories on a cozy daytime talk show sofa.

There was a time in the campaign history that daytime talk shows were seen more as a platform for entertainment than a platform for political campaign communication; they were not perceived as acceptable forums for candidates. Late-night talk shows were seen as adversarial, low brow, and risky campaign stops. When Arkansas Governor Bill Clinton appeared on the *Arsenio Hall Show* in 1992, donning Rat Pack style sunglasses and jamming Elvis' "Heartbreak Hotel" on the saxophone, reactions were mixed. It was novel – yet strange – to see a candidate for president fully embrace the affordances of entertainment media. In other words, "What was *he* doing *there*?!" Some criticized Clinton for what they perceived as unprofessional conduct, belittling the office he sought. Others celebrated the novelty, characterizing Clinton as cool, relatable, and refreshing.

Alas, much has changed in the media landscape and, consequently, the campaign process. Today's candidates no longer treat entertainment media as an optional or novel part of the campaign process; engaging with entertainment media is now an imperative for candidates – even among those seeking

DOI: 10.4324/9781003364832-1

the highest level of public office. Take for example GOP presidential candidate Carly Fiorina singing a folksy jingle about her pet dog on *The Tonight Show* with Jimmy Fallon in 2016, or Kamala Harris directly tweeting at Maya Rudolph to publicly applaud the comedian for her *SNL* impersonation of the then congresswoman. The late Senator John McCain made multiple appearances on *SNL* in 2008, and, during his presidency, Barack Obama adopted dry, deadpan humor to promote the Affordable Care Act on digital comedy program, *Between Two Ferns*. There is, of course, Donald Trump's aggressive and entertaining use of Twitter that helped catapult him to the White House in 2016. More recently, former New York Mayor Michael Bloomberg even hired social media strategists from the notorious Fyre music festival to manage his campaign memes when running for president in 2020. (Fortunately, Bloomberg stopped short of putting rapper Ja Rule on the campaign payroll.) And Congresswoman Alexandria Ocasio-Cortez unabashedly embraced the opportunity to serve as guest judge for RuPaul's *Drag Race* that same year. Indeed, much has changed in the arena of presidential campaigns.

Political elites and candidates for even the highest levels of public office now understand that engagement with entertainment media is non-negotiable – and for good reason. Much has changed in the media landscape over the past five decades, and today's campaigns must understand that if they are to have a fighting chance to maintain relevancy and reach an inattentive electorate, consistent engagement with entertainment media is critical. Before exploring the strategic campaign implications of this new norm, this chapter will first unpack the key developments across mass media to help us understand the dramatic shift in how candidates have reduced or replaced time spent with traditional news media to embrace these popular platforms that were initially intended for public entertainment rather than political engagement.

Decisions, decisions: the media's "long tail"

Media consumers today choose from an abundance of streaming choices including Netflix, YouTube, Apple TV, Disney Plus, Hulu, and more. What we watch, when we watch, and how we watch have increasingly become less predictable. But when your professors were in college, they could often predict what their friends were doing at certain evening hours based on network airtime of popular programs. For example, many college students were glued to their television sets each Wednesday night for CBS' *Survivor*. To watch, viewers would need to set aside the same day and time each week to ensure that they wouldn't miss which castaway would get the boot. This form of media consumption, based on an established schedule, is what is known as an **appointment model** of media consumption. Viewers would anxiously wait for each episode's release at a specific day and time each week, eagerly anticipating the next plot turn and dramatic development. Scheduling television time seems archaic and laborious today given the abundance of streaming options and the limitless ways we access media – from computers to tablets, mobile devices, and even gaming consoles. Who even needs a television set these days?!

What you are more accustomed to today is a form of consumption introduced by streaming powerhouse Netflix, which pioneered the **binge model** of media consumption. This format not only allowed consumers to choose when they wanted to watch their programs but also allowed them to control the pace of viewing. In 2013, Netflix released entire seasons of its first hit programs *Orange Is the New Black* and *House of Cards*, allowing media consumers to go on a viewing bender of sorts. And the content could even be viewed on a home computer, a mobile device, or tablet. Most young people are quite accustomed to such flexibility in when and how they consume media. Nonetheless, this abundance of choice is also quite necessary in understanding shifts in campaign norms. It wasn't too long ago where U.S. audiences were limited in what they consume, when they consume, and how they consume media.

The term **mass media** describes an environment built on attracting large, diverse audiences. Content was created by a handful of mega companies for general audiences, with the intent of widespread, mass appeal. The U.S. media landscape could be characterized as a mass media environment for several decades following the introduction of the steam powered printing press in 1814, through radio and network television's golden years. From news to entertainment, from books and magazines to radio programs, dramas, and sitcoms, content was produced, marketed, and delivered for broad audiences. And media companies did so successfully due to limited options for entertainment relative to what consumers have access to today, and thanks to the appointment model in which media companies had all the leverage in how and when audiences would consume content.

In the context of television, consumers had four national networks to pick from: ABC, CBS, NBC, and later FOX. The electorate was consuming news programs at the same hours of the day, provided by a small elite group of corporations, and consuming entertaining programming at similar hours of the day provided by that same core of media companies. In other words, consumption habits were rather predictable by design. This mass media environment is sometimes referred to as **the short head**, meaning that audiences were sizable and consuming the same few programs from a short list of content providers. Audiences had access to limited media options and media choice. Until one small company slowly developed a ripple in the market that would result in a fracturing of the "mass" audience and a sea change for how the electorate consumes media. If you're one of the 16 million viewing fans of *Euphoria*, you most certainly know of this disruptor of a company.

In 1975, a little-known cable access provider connecting a small market of people in remote areas to community antenna television (so that they could receive a signal to view the big four networks on their home television sets) lobbied the Federal Communications Commission to operate not only as a cable access provider for those in rural areas but also as a content creator.

HBO wanted to expand its operations to include the distribution of its own in-house programming. Unthreatened by HBO's meager size and the small market share that relied on the company for community antenna television, the major networks didn't challenge the move. But the ease of installing home satellite dishes helped generate new interest in the cable market, and after HBO, others followed suit. Businessman Ted Turner launched TBS and CNN. In the years following, cable welcomed BET, Nickelodeon, ESPN, and MTV. These new channels offered consumers a variety of entertaining content, and while they shared almost nothing in common in terms of the programs they distributed, they were bound by one important characteristic that would, collectively, disrupt the mass media environment. Each cable channel catered to a narrowly targeted audience. Cable television marked the emergence of a new media environment known as **the long tail** or an environment characterized by an abundance of media choices with smaller fragmented audiences.

In a 2004 article published in *Wired* magazine, Chris Anderson coined this media landscape as the long tail, meaning that distribution of audiences was now fragmented across multiple media products, platforms, and outlets. This era defined by an abundance of media choice was a slow evolution that began with the new options provided by cable television but amplified further as homes began connecting to the internet in the 1990s. Anderson (2006) would go on to pen a book about this new environment of media abundance, describing it as a departure from mass media collectively consumed by large diverse audiences replaced instead by consumption habits that are far more individualistic and niche. In other words, we were consuming more media in this long-tail environment, but we were far less likely to be consuming the *same* media.

In a short head environment, if you were disinterested in network television, you could pick up a book or listen to FM radio. If you were uninterested in mainstream news, you could possibly turn to some alternative weeklies, but audiences were quite trapped in the mainstream without many alternatives. If you dislike today's mainstream news, you can easily find information else-where – blogs, websites, and social media. If the sitcoms and serial dramas on the big four networks bore you, have no fear as dozens of streaming options await you. The long tail disrupted not only audience's consumption habits but also the very economic structures that allow commercial media companies to thrive. In this environment of choice, companies no longer need to generate mass appeal or a smash hit show. In the long tail, content can be successful in spaces inhabited by narrow, well-defined audiences and small-scale distribution. Media companies can take more risks and move from the center toward more partisan news or toward entertainment that might be considered an acquired taste or envelope-pushing. A loyal niche audience can even revive a show through a digital crowdfunding campaign – just ask the fans of the *Veronica Mars* series or *Super Troopers 2*. Regardless of how cult or obscure the following may be, content can find a devoted audience in the long tail.

Your tastes no longer need to be mainstream for media companies to see you, hear you, and cater to you.

Fragmentation of the audience for entertainment might sound rather empowering and darn convenient. But how does the long tail affect the news business and news consumption? For better or worse, the era of media defined by the mass audience had shifted to fragmented, niche audiences and that meant that the monopoly network news had on the nightly attention of the electorate was no more.

Cable television and the fall of network news

Today, *NBC Nightly News* with Lester Holt is the second ranked news program in the country, attracting approximately eight million viewers, according to Nielsen. Nonetheless, in a classroom of about 40 college students, only three could identify the headshot of Holt. Living in the long tail, this anecdote should not surprise us. Although eight million sounds like a sizable audience in today's ubiquitous media environment, that figure is about half of what it used to be.

On a typical evening in the 1960s and 1970s, about 75% of homes with their television sets on would be tuned in to the nightly news, and an even greater percentage for local news programs (Prior, 2007, p. 71). In truth, there was little else for Americans to tune in to at the time. When audiences were later surveyed about their preferences for news and entertainment, 79.9% of those with only access to network television preferred consuming news, whereas just 35.4% of those who had access to both network *and* cable television preferred news (Prior, 2007, p. 35). Given the choice, it seems audiences would rather abandon the news for more entertaining options – and they did. Let's consider data tracked by Nielsen. Viewership for nightly news programs across networks CBS, ABC, and NBC averaged around 52 million viewers a night in 1980, around 41 million viewers in 1990, and just 32 million viewers in 2000 (Pew, 2015). When home adoption rates ticked upwards in the early 1980s, as cable providers ramped up their entertainment offerings, the audience for network news plummeted. Although Prior (2007) noted that network news viewership remained relatively stable through the mid-1990s for homes without a cable subscription, even those homes began to experience a decline in news viewership as the internet accelerated trends in audience fragmentation.

It's not often that you hear people applauding television for its benefits to democracy these days, but there was a time when the medium was touted as a useful tool for educating the public. Research had indicated that network television acted as a knowledge leveler of sorts, helping to catch up low information voters in learning about politics. This incidental learning was largely a result of the short head media environment. From the 1950s through the early 1980s, the major networks relished their captive audiences. Family members would return from school and work and could choose between a handful of local and national news programming across the networks; the sitcoms and dramas wouldn't begin airing until 8 p.m., the start of prime time for advertising and viewership. For these set pre-dinner hours, disengaging with news called for disengaging with the medium altogether, but Americans were rarely willing to turn off the tube. It was our collective love of the television – not news – that kept us glued to those informative news programs (Prior, 2007). Of course, cable changed all that in the 1980s, giving audiences their first taste of a long-tail media environment with bundled content. But all that media choice came at a steep price.

The expansion of cable meant new challenges for network television, creating a media landscape that scholar Markus Prior refers to as "**post-broadcast democracy.**" Prior's work (2005, 2007) demonstrated that the abundance of media provided by cable fragmented audiences and chipped away at public attentiveness to news. His research suggests that news audiences were cut by about half after the introduction of cable, suggesting that Americans' interest in news was overstated in the network era of television, because choice was limited and network programming schedules were uniform, leaving audiences with little opportunity to opt out of local and national news (Prior, 2005). In other words, cable offered the electorate a way to shift its attention from politicians and news to entertainment (Baum & Kernell, 1999). What cable showed us was that audiences weren't tuning in to news programs for love of current events but because that was the only type of content provided during those hours of the day. It was love for the medium of television that kept audiences tuned in.

In a long-tail environment, audiences exude more control over their media consumption habits, but when given a choice, most will choose entertainment over news. Media abundance may provide the electorate with more agencies, but all these choices also disengage much of the electorate from the democratic process.

After the emergence of cable and, later, the web, Prior (2007) found a **knowledge gap** between news seekers and entertainment seekers, along with the gap in voter turnout. This means that those who were gravitating to entertainment media over news were becoming less informed and more detached from the political process. In other words, the incidental exposure to network news in the short head environment simply wasn't happening in the long tail. Prior also found that people with middle-of-the-road views were gravitating to entertainment media at higher rates than people who were identified as partisan, meaning that moderate voters were becoming especially inattentive to news and less involved in the political process. Thus, media choice is somewhat responsible for the intensified political polarization of today as moderate thinkers increasingly disengage.

An abundance of media choice not only lured audiences from news programs to entertainment but also fragmented audiences across various news sources. Cable television and the web offered various delivery styles and formats for news, alternatives to the more objective models of mainstream outlets. News consumption habits were more individualistic. People began self-selecting news sources, gravitating to those more aligned with their existing predispositions and political beliefs. This process, often referred to as **selective exposure**, suggests that in today's environment of media abundance, audiences easily consume media aligned with their own political ideology and resist more objective news sources that may challenge existing beliefs and values. And as media became more portable, consumers engaged with news more superficially, becoming **news grazers** that read headlines, surf news channels, and skim through the first couple of paragraphs of an article (Morris & Forgette, 2007).

Scholars were encouraged by the democratizing effects of the broadcast era, as limited choice and network news programs helped boost knowledge for low information voters. But those effects eroded in the environment of media abundance (Gurevitch et al., 2009). As audiences fragmented and dispersed across various media, the death of the mass audience made it increasingly difficult for campaigns in the long tail to reach large swaths of the electorate. Audience fragmentation has also strained the relationship between news outlets and their audiences. Audience fragmentation also correlated with steep declines in public trust of mainstream news organizations, making it difficult for candidates to connect with voters through mainstream media.

The growing disdain for mainstream news

The fragmented media audience means that people are so inundated with sources of information today that they are more dismissive of traditional news outlets. In today's public discourse, it is so en vogue to call news media biased that it is borderline cliché. Much of the public hostility toward news professionals, and the outlets that employ them, can be attributed to the long tail and our limitless options of information sources. Public trust in the era of media abundance has fallen to historic lows. According to Gallup, just 36% of Americans today have a great deal or fair amount of trust in the media, marking the second lowest level of trust since 1972, when the pollster began measuring public trust in the press (Brenan, 2021). Throughout the 1970s, Gallup reported that public trust in the news media fluctuated between 68% and 72%. As the media environment fragmented over the next three decades, that figure would be reduced by more than half, as just 32% of respondents reported trusting the media in 2016 (Brenan, 2021). And those who were identified as Republican exhibit even greater levels of distrust for mainstream news.

Data from the National Election Studies have shown that declines in news trust have coincided with increasing household adoption rates of cable and worsened with the addition of the internet (Prior, 2007). Ladd (2011) has argued that increasing competition in the news industry intensified the problem of eroding public trust. The fragmented, high-choice media environment paved the way for more entertaining and interpretive styles of news production, sensationalism, and news negativity. The high-choice media environment offered numerous escapes and more entertaining options, and for news organizations to compete for attention, news and entertainment would need to blur. Cable news introduced more biased perspectives, interpretive news, and conflict-driven programs with heated bickering and partisan hot takes – anything that might heighten the entertainment value of news. Fox News exploited a market for an agenda-driven model of news production, serving as a cable news mouthpiece for conservative views, whereas MSNBC adopted a similar, yet more subdued style, for delivering liberally biased news. Meanwhile, cable network Comedy Central devoted considerable airtime to satirical news programs such as *The Daily Show* and *The Colbert Report*, amplifying public cynicism toward mainstream news.

One consequence of these entertaining shifts in news content is audiences that perceive the media as the media too powerful, too negative, and untrustworthy. These public perceptions make audiences less attentive to mainstream news and more attentive to biased sources of information (Tsfati & Cappella, 2003). Historically considered a crucial check and balance to U.S. democracy, the public now holds unfavorable views of the news "institution" (Gronke & Cook, 2007; Ladd, 2011). Today's credibility problem is no longer confined to conservatives perceiving liberal media bias; trust of mainstream news is widespread across the political spectrum (Ladd, 2013). A concerning trend given that trust in news professionals makes people more likely to consume news (Williams, 2012). A decline in news trust means a decline in attentiveness to mainstream media, and these patterns hold implications for where voters turn to for news and information.

Today's fragmented media environment and the inclination toward selective exposure mean that people are especially distrusting of news outlets perceived as incongruent with their political predispositions (Arceneaux et al., 2012). Selective exposure is closely related to how audiences assess media bias. Researchers identified a **hostile media effect**, a belief among people that mainstream media is often biased against their personal ideology, political party, or preferred candidate (Vallone et al., 1985). Feldman's (2011) work noted that people's perceptions of news bias depend heavily on whether a news outlet's slant is congruent with one's beliefs. When news outlets provide biased content that reflects our own ideological leanings, we are less likely to perceive bias; thus, the fragmented environment is posing new challenges in the public's ability to fairly evaluate the creditability of a news organization. Declining public trust in news not only makes people gravitate to more partisan news sources but also makes its audiences more resistant to objective news coverage (Ladd, 2011, 2013).

The long tail ushered in an era of public distrust for mainstream news and drove audiences to blogs, websites, podcasts, and slanted cable news programs that are often united in their skepticism of mainstream news and quick to abandon the aspirational journalistic objectivity. These less traditional sources of news tend to deliver information with increased incivility, which may not only provide click bait or help television ratings but also push middle-of-the road voters away from news as they perceive political coverage as being too conflict driven (Mutz & Reeves, 2005). And with its algorithms that feed users polarized and ideologically biased content, social media has only intensified the public's distrust for mainstream news.

The web has enhanced the ease in which audiences can engage in selective exposure and carefully curate their news diets to align with their political views and world beliefs. Social media has also helped to mainstream propaganda and misinformation campaigns. For example, in the months ramping up to the 2016 U.S. presidential election, a Buzzfeed analysis revealed that Facebook users had more engagement with fake news stories than stories published by legitimate news outlets (Silverman, 2016). Algorithms tailored to preexisting biases of the end user have helped to create digital **echo chambers** where people are closed off to diverse viewpoints and balanced perspectives. This is especially troubling given that more people are using social media as their primary or, in some cases, only source of news. According to Pew, roughly half of U.S. adults now consume news on social media platforms (Walker & Matsa, 2021). Moreover, news articles shared by peers on social media are often perceived as more credible than when the same article is shared directly from a reputable news outlet (Turcotte et al., 2015).

Although there is little evidence to support systemic bias in mainstream journalism, often defined as the consistent intrusion of reporter ideology, the perception of bias is as damning as actual bias. The perception of bias, whether real or imagined, pushes people toward fringe or heavily partisan sources of information. For others, the shouting matches and us-versus-them coverage disengages audiences altogether, further pushing them toward entertainment media as a form of escapism. When news audiences are increasingly fragmented and disengaged from politics, campaigns must work even harder to access potential voters. In the "post-broadcast democracy," campaigns must move on from mainstream news media. If candidates for public office are to reach voters, they need to reimagine the campaign process and engage with content and platforms that had once been considered beneath politics.

Goals of this text

Politicians have long resisted campaigning through entertainment media, but as media choice exploded, it is now imperative that candidates leverage new tools to reach voters. Public discourse that would historically have transpired on the newsprint of opinion pages or behind a news anchor's desk and teleprompter now happens on sitcoms, memes, influencer accounts, video games, and social media. The seminal texts in political communication understate the role entertainment media play in shaping campaigns and policymaking strategies. Other works published on this intersection of entertainment and politics have almost exclusively focused on the effects of entertainment media on civic outcomes such as voter knowledge and political engagement.

This text examines the shift from campaigning predominantly through the news media to campaigning through entertainment media and demonstrates how evolving media consumption habits have shaped campaign norms and shifted strategies for winning elections and advancing policy goals. Now we have a solid understanding of key shifts in the media landscape; we may now examine how this evolution to the long tail cemented new campaign norms – norms that would require candidates to fully embrace and even prioritize entertainment media as campaign strategy.

Chapter previews

Chapter 2, provides an additional foundation for understanding the modern campaign and the critical role entertainment media play in shaping those campaigns. This chapter examines the ways in which the news media treat elections as entertainment, sport, and spectacle. The chapter addresses how the news media cover political campaigns and the shift in discourse treating politicians as "celebrity" and their supporters as "fans." Chapter 2 unpacks the commodification of political campaigns realized through consumer marketing strategies, further underscoring this association with politicians as commodity-celebrity and voters as consumer-fans.

The text shifts to its strategic communication focus by examining one of the earliest forms of entertainment media utilized on the campaign trail. Chapter 3 explores how entertainment programs emerged, albeit slowly, as a relevant campaign tool. This chapter examines strategic use of daytime talk shows and late-night television platforms that have enabled candidates to introduce themselves to the American public, reach inattentive voters, and enhance public perceptions of relatability and trustworthiness.

Chapter 4 moves beyond infotainment programs to programs entirely focused on audience amusement. The notion of candidates making cameo appearances on entertainment programs was relatively rare during network television's golden years. Newt Gingrich's 1996 cameo on Murphy Brown was teased for nearly a year leading up to the episode, reinforcing the novelty of this marriage between entertainment and politics. As audiences began to abandon news for entertainment, the stigma associated with cameos began to fade, essentially reducing the political risks of candidate appearances in comedic formats. From John McCain to Joe Biden, cameos are now a common component of campaign strategy that improves a politician's relatability, generates news, and lets candidates connect with voters.

It is not a particularly well-kept secret that politicians and celebrities have been odd bedfellows. Hollywood's influence on politics has a rich history, but what has changed is that the relationship between the two has moved to the public domain. Thus, Chapter 5 explores the evolution from private celebrity support to highly visible public endorsements and partnerships that generate national headlines, flood our social media feeds, and trickle down to the convention stages. This chapter goes beyond the private fundraising galas and role celebrities historically played in the campaign process to examine how campaigns court celebrity influence, particularly in the social media environment.

Of course, no text focused on strategic use of entertainment media in campaign politics is worth its salt unless it grapples with the ever-changing digital platforms at a candidate's disposal. Chapter 6 examines novel campaign uses of digital and social media to demonstrate their functionality as both campaign and fundraising tools. Chapter 6 not only unpacks the 2004 Howard Dean campaign's use of Meetup.com and Barack Obama's partnership with a Facebook cofounder but also explores more innovative strategies from the rising use of meme campaigns, digital shorts, influencers, streams, and video games to demonstrate how campaigns have reimagined digital spaces as campaign tools.

Finally, this book will consider the democratic implications of today's entertainment-driven campaigns and ponder the future role such media will play in the electoral process. Is anything off limits? How will future disruptions in the media landscape continue to shape political campaign communication? Regardless, of what is in store for the marriage between entertainment media and campaigns, Chapter 7 examines the affordances and limitations to campaigning through entertainment media. This concluding chapter provides an overview of normative arguments related to the intersection of entertainment media and politics and assesses potential civic benefits while predicting future manifestations of entertainment media use within political campaign communication.

Ultimately, the argument this text delivers is not that these campaign trends are inherently beneficial or problematic to democracy, but, rather, these trends are non-negotiable, now deeply embedded within campaign strategy, and are quite directly dictated by the evolution of the long tail and dramatic changes in the media consumption habits of the U.S. electorate.

Resources and references

Anderson, C. (2006). *The long tail*. Hyperion.

Arceneaux, K., Johnson, M., & Murphy, C. (2012). Polarized political communication, oppositional media hostility, and selective exposure. *Journal of Politics, 74*(1), 174–186.

Baum, M. A., & Kernell, S. (1999). Has cable ended the golden age of presidential television? *American Political Science Review, 93*, 99–114.

Brenan, M. (2021). Americans trust in media dips to second lowest on record. *Gallup*. Retrieved May 28, 2022, from https://news.gallup.com/poll/355526/americans-trust-media-dips-second-lowest-record.aspx

Feldman, L. (2011). Partisan differences in opinionated news perceptions: A test of the hostile media effect. *Political Behavior, 33*, 407–432.

Gronke, P., & Cook, T. (2007). Disdaining the media: The American public's changing attitudes toward the news. *Political Communication, 24*(3), 259–281.

Gurevitch, M., Coleman, S., & Blumler, J. G. (2009). Political communication: Old and new media relationships. *The Annals of the American Academy of Political and Social Science, 625*(1), 164–181.

Ladd, J. M. (2011). *Why Americans hate the media and how it matters.* Princeton University Press.

Ladd, J. M. (2013). The era of media distrust and its consequences for perceptions of political reality. In T. N. Ridout (Ed.), *New directions in media and politics* (pp. 24–44). Routledge.

Morris, J. S., & Forgette, R. (2007). News grazers, television news, political knowledge, and engagement. *Harvard International Journal of Press/Politics, 12*(1), 91–107.

Mutz, D. C., & Reeves, B. (2005). The new videomalaise: Effects of televised incivility on political trust. *American Political Science Review, 99*(1), 1–16.

Pew. (2015, July 9). Network TV: Evening news overall viewership since 1980. Pew Research Center. https://www.pewresearch.org/journalism/chart/network-tv-evening-news-overall-viewership-since-1980/.

Prior, M. (2005). News vs. entertainment: How increasing media choice widens gaps in political knowledge and turnout. *American Journal of Political Science, 49*(3), 577–592.

Prior, M. (2007). *Post-broadcast democracy: How media choice increase inequality in political involvement and polarizes elections.* Cambridge University Press.

Silverman, J. (2016). This analysis shows how viral fake news election stories outperformed real news on Facebook. *Buzzfeed News.*

Tsfati, Y., & Cappella, J. N. (2003). Do people watch what they do not trust? Exploring the association between news media skepticism and exposure. *Communication Research, 30*(5), 504–529.

Turcotte, J., York, C., Irving, J., Scholl, R. M., & Pingree, R. J. (2015). News recommendations from social media opinion leaders: Effects on media trust and information seeking. *Journal of Computer-Mediated Communication, 20*(5), 520–535.

Vallone, R. P., Ross, L., & Lepper, M. R. (1985). The hostile media phenomenon: Biased perception and perceptions of media bias in coverage of the Beirut massacre. *Journal of Personality and Social Psychology, 49*(3), 577–585.

Walker, M., & Matsa, K. E. (2021). *News consumption across social media in 2021.* Pew Research Center. Retrieved May 28, 2022, from https://www.pewresearch.org/journalism/2021/09/20/news-consumption-across-social-media-in-2021/

Williams, A. E. (2012). Trust or bust? Questioning the relationship between media trust and news attention. *Journal of Broadcasting & Electronic Media, 56*(1), 116–131.

2 Merch, fandom, and sports metaphors

The commodification of the modern campaign

Standing before a crowd at the 1956 Democratic National Convention in Chicago, nominee Adlai Stevenson looked to galvanize the party ahead of the general election. He also voiced his disgust with the campaign process. "The idea that you can merchandise candidates for high office like breakfast cereal – that you can gather votes like box tops – is, I think, the ultimate indignity to the democratic process" (Stevenson, 1956). The former Illinois governor did not go on to win the presidency, but his acceptance speech lived on as a cautionary warning about political campaigns that is especially prescient today: the commercialization of the electoral process. Stevenson's appeal fell on deaf ears.

Also present during that convention speech was U.S. Senator Lyndon B. Johnson, a challenger to Stevenson who failed to earn the nomination of the Democratic Party in 1956. Two election cycles later, Johnson would expand the influence of consumer marketing techniques in presidential politics with his campaign's hiring of advertising firm Doyle Dane Bernbach – a firm that helped sell brand image and consumer products for clients such as Volkswagen and Quaker Oats (Mann, 2016). The firm's notorious "daisy girl" spot ad that ran for 60 seconds on network television for Johnson's 1964 campaign escalated the role that consumer marketing played in political campaign communication and signaled a shift from policy-driven ads to the emotion-based appeals common in the advertising of consumer goods. In other words, the commodification of the contemporary campaign was now underway.

Rethinking presidential candidates as a commodity or good and political parties as a brand may have been an inevitable consequence of an industrialized, capitalist society but that thinking also expedited the blurring between entertainment and politics and normalized Stevenson's "box top" campaign fears. This chapter continues to unpack the commodification of campaigns by documenting shifts in how the news media cover elections, examining why celebrities increasingly emerge as candidates, and exploring campaign use of consumer marketing strategies that treat candidates as celebrities and products and voters as fans and consumers.

DOI: 10.4324/9781003364832-2

Campaigns as news spectacles

The news media, sometimes referred to as the "Fourth Estate," serves a democratic function by informing the public and conveying timely and fact-checked information that helps people make sense of the world and reach political decisions. But first and foremost, the news media is a for-profit enterprise and news is a commodity or product. To best understand the spectacle of election coverage, let us first unpack some of the challenges facing newsrooms in the era of media abundance and consider how market-driven news production ultimately contributes to the commodification of campaigns.

Research has shown that as competitive market pressures increase for a news organization, coverage prioritizes softer entertaining news content (Hamilton, 2004; Dunaway, 2008). News outlets cater content to demographics deemed profitable by advertisers and introduce more entertaining formats by adopting interpretive styles of delivery that satisfies profit pressures in a competitive media environment. In other words, "infotainment" is the modern newsroom's response to media abundance and fragmentation, because it helps to retain audiences. The ratings chase, so to speak, influences content considerations. This highly competitive market prioritizes news as a marketable commodity or product above all else. Although news organizations have always had to satisfy a healthy profit margin, a more competitive and fragmented environment only heightens emphasis on consumer-driven models of news production. The result is that news organizations are increasingly adopting a "give the people want they want" approach to news production.

These commercial interests partly explain the explosion in campaign **horserace coverage**, as these news narratives focused on electability or which candidates are ahead and behind in an election are more entertaining to audiences (Iyengar et al., 2004). It is common for horserace coverage to account for close to half of all election news content. In a study analyzing the 2008 presidential election, scholars found that horserace stories accounted for nearly half of all election news content, with online news sources yielding an even higher volume of this frame (Belt et al., 2012). During the 2016 U.S. presidential election, horserace frames accounted for 43% of the news media's election coverage, relative to just 10% focused on policy issues (Patterson, 2016). These horserace stories also reflect a rise in polling data, enhancing the ease with which journalists can report on the competitive aspects of an election.

The horserace also affects news coverage of other critical political events, from political debates to even state of the union addresses, with journalists focused on performance and which politician or party scores the most points with voters. Even coverage of policy issues is often laced with horserace frames, focusing on the competitive aspects of legislating and what political parties stand to gain or lose. This type of policy coverage is often referred to as **game-frames** (Lawrence, 2000). But when journalists focus on the competitive aspects of politics, it results in less news attention to policy (Patterson, 2016; Turcotte, 2017).

Another important trend in the spectacle of campaign news is the increasing level of media hostility on the campaign trail, with the tone of coverage skewing more negative in recent decades (Farnsworth & Lichter, 2011). And much of this negativity is a consequence of more interpretive and entertaining styles of reporting the news. The more aggressively toned news results in more competitive news frames and a heightened perception of political polarization. The continuous news focus on strategy and winning may also fuel greater perception of the **hostile media effect**, a theory rooted in psychological research examining the phenomenon of sports fandom. The hostile media effect is a finding that shows that partisan people often perceive the news media as biased against their own political ideology or party (Vallone et al., 1985). In the same vein that die-hard fans hold refs accountable when their team loses, strong partisans blame electoral losses on biased or unfair treatment from the media.

And as the data behind political campaigns have become more robust, journalists and pollsters utilize sports rhetoric to contextualize horserace coverage and election forecasts with increasing regularity (Butterworth, 2014). Even the most renowned election forecaster, Nate Silver, founder of *FiveThityEight*, began his career not as a political forecaster but as a statistician forecasting baseball and developing sports prediction modeling. But the horserace news frame is just one of the manifestations of treating news as a commercial good. The language that both news professionals and political elites use to characterize campaigns and policymaking permeate our political discourse and rewires us to think of political parties and politicians not as institutions and public officials but as teams, celebrities, and brands.

The framing of politics as sport

Shortly after President Obama's reelection to a second term in the White House, members of Congress had to confront a looming policy debate head on as several federal tax breaks were scheduled to sunset at the end of 2012, leaving $65 billion in spending cuts on the horizon for the new year. That much loss in revenue for federal programs would place Washington careening toward what some economists described as a "fiscal cliff." In December 2012, neither party made much progress reaching compromise over spending. Senate majority leader Harry Reid's solution? Take to the Senate floor to compare Republican leadership to the New York Jets – an NFL team that, according to friends of mine, is notoriously bad and bumbling.

Reid, a Democrat from Utah, opened his Senate remarks by addressing the stalemate with Republican members of Congress over a policy response to the "fiscal cliff," by criticizing party leadership. Reid said:

> Coach Ryan, he's got a problem. He has three quarterbacks: Sanchez, he's got Tim Tebow, he's got a guy by the name of McElroy. He can't decide who their quarterback is going to be. That's the same problem the Republicans

are having. Romney's gone but he's still in the background. We have McConnell and we have Boehner. Who is the quarterback, Mr. President? Who is the quarterback?

Unsurprisingly, Senate minority leader Mitch McConnell, a Republican from Kentucky, fired back with continued sports rhetoric. McConnell quipped:

> The majority leader points out that there is some confusion on who the quarterback is on the Republican side . . . there's no question who the quarterback is on the Democratic side; it's President Obama, and he keeps throwing interceptions.

The exchange is emblematic of the sports rhetoric takeover over contemporary political discourse. Whether it's the news media's preoccupation with the horse race, "front runners," and underdogs or the framing of policy debates through sports metaphors and analogies, the discourse diminishes the stakes and likens democracy to a game.

Although there were concerns of the news media treating politics as spectacle long before media's long tail, the increasing influence of election forecasting, pollsters, and cable television intensified sports rhetoric in politics due to endless opining, interpreting, and predicting that transpired on 24-hour news networks (Sigelman & Bullock, 2016). Predictions would come earlier and earlier with each election cycle, long before some candidates would formally launch their campaigns. Pundits with one foot in Washington and skin in the game would heighten the competitive aspects of campaign politics and create a binary back-and-forth or shouting match on cable news programs. Even the news coverage and discourse of campaign debates, important for educating voters, are reduced to the language of sport, competition, and candidate *performance*. Sports rhetoric also permeates print media. For example, one of *Politico*'s newsletters is aptly named "Playbook." *The Hill*, a D.C.-based publication, routinely uses terms such as "the game" and "the field" to describe campaign politics. The persistent narrative of gamesmanship also affects the discourse political elites use to campaign and govern.

Many of us are familiar with the jargon associated with one or more sports. We may turn in a school assignment thinking it was a "home run" or "slam dunk" or consider an act of inter-office diplomacy "well played." News professionals *and* politicians deploy the language of sport so routinely that it now shapes how policy is communicated to the public. Among the popular sports metaphors reaching political discourse are home stretch, front-runner, game-changer, playbook, step up to the plate, home run, slam dunk, and touchdown. Jargon associated with baseball and football is especially popular for politicians to engage low information voters in policy understanding. The rhetorical strategy simplifies politics through American pastimes, scoring big on patriotic appeals.

President Bush was not only an avid runner but also a fan of baseball. In fact, Bush's investment in the Texas Rangers in 1989 eventually landed him the title of general managing partner of the organization. Throughout his two terms, Bush favored jargon associated with jogging and baseball – two of his passions. Moreover, the Bush administration routinely deployed sports metaphors to communicate policy to the media and the public. Sports jargon included phrases like "sprint to the finish" and "time on the clock," along with "marathon" and "quarter" metaphors. "Touch downs" and "home runs" were used by Vice President Dick Cheney to characterize the administration's progress in Afghanistan (AP, 2007). Although Bush was the first president to adopt the language of sport with such regularity, President Obama continued the trend during his two terms in office.

Despite basketball being his preferred sport, Obama looked to football when addressing the shortcomings of the Affordable Care Act rollout. When the Healthcare.gov website launched in 2013, Americans were met with crashes, long wait times, and frustration. Obama addressed the nation from the White House that November, likening the rollout blunders to a "fumble" (Decker, 2013). He boiled the issue down to a performance problem, promising he would make the right "play" next time. In December 2019, during an appearance on *Face the Nation*, Democrat Chris Coons turned to sports analogies in his criticism of President Trump's foreign policy. Coons derided Trump's decision to withdraw troops from Syria, believing that it threatened U.S. progress on defeating ISIS. He added, "We shouldn't fumble the ball on the five-yard line." Republican Senator Lindsey Graham chimed in with a counter statement on Syria during a CNN interview, delivering yet another yard line analogy.

While the Bush administration played an important role in normalizing the language of sport in politics, the last few election cycles have shown that political elites from all ideological spectrums have embraced the rhetoric. One possible strategic explanation is that research shows that both liberals and conservatives are equally as likely to follow sports and engage in sports fandom (Thorson & Serazio, 2018). In other words, in a divisive and polarizing political climate, politicians can play it safe using sports rhetoric that appeals to a broad swath of voters without the worry of alienating a particular ideological group. Moreover, the infiltration of sports in electoral politics goes beyond rhetoric. Visual cues, music, and promotional teasers for election events have adopted all the pomp and circumstance of televised sports coverage.

With Fox News and MSNBC building audiences by catering to politically slanted coverage, the playing-it-down-the-middle approach has left CNN scrambling for market scraps. Critics have noted the network's strong pull toward sports-like packaging of political news. When the network hosted a 2019 U.S. presidential primary debate, viewers were met with a dramatic start as the network introduced candidates with as much zest as a WWF pro wrestler. Hollywood trailer style promotional videos, teasers, and candidate biographies surprised media critics and viewers alike during CNN coverage of the 2020 debates sponsored by the network. CNN was accused of packaging campaign news in a style that rivaled *American Ninja Warrior*, with dramatic music and voiceover (Moran, 2019). That same year, CNN drew heat for broadcasting an elaborate game of randomized ping pong balls to determine the placement of candidates in a primary debate. The footage showed multiple CNN anchors shuffling candidate cards in a drawn-out, dramatic fashion with multiple camera views. CNN was accused of turning the debates into a "circus" and "game show." The format resembled a striking similarity to the NBA's draft lottery process.

Vox (2017) attributed much of CNN's treatment of politics as competitive sport to leadership that came not from a news background but from entertainment television. Jeff Zucker joined CNN as president in 2013, after building an extensive resume in show business. Formerly the president of NBC Entertainment, Zucker, was credited with inking Donald Trump to the reality show *The Apprentice* and greenlighting *Fear Factor*. Building his resume on competitive reality television game shows, CNN's path toward sports-like political coverage was perhaps a reflection of Zucker's leadership and the network's political programming included over-the-top countdown clocks, dramatic music, pulsating graphics, and promotional teasers. And the network's shouting match brand of programming was starting to mirror ESPN's aggressive sports programs like *First Take*. The treatment of politics as sport permeates other mainstream news networks and even online and print media. Consequently, it also primes audiences to take elections less seriously.

The emphasis on sports jargon can prime voters to feel more like passive spectators and fans rather than active and engaged participants of democracy (Martinez, 2015). Over time, sports rhetoric elevates politicians to celebrity status, akin to athletes competing for and representing their team. And the "team" in this analogy is their political party. The language of sport certainly holds implications for the polarizing nature of politics, especially given what we have learned about the hostile media effect. While it may be good for television ratings, the perception of politics as a game contributes to declining levels of public trust in politicians and democratic institutions and increasing polarization and cynicism.

According to Gallup, only 36% of Americans reported having a "great deal" or "fair amount" of trust in the news media in 2021, marking the second lowest figure since the pollster began measuring institutional trust in 1972 (Brenan, 2021). In fact, that figure has not eclipsed the 50% mark since 2003, demonstrating a steady erosion in public trust in news outlets in today's ubiquitous media environment. Pew reports that in 2001, about 50% of Americans said that they trust the government to do what is right "always" or "most of the time" but that figure dropped dramatically, fluctuating between 17% and 24% during the Trump and Biden presidencies (Pew, 2022). Americans may not be entirely disengaged from democracy but are, however, treating it less seriously and feeling more cynical about it. When the news media, political elites, and the public take its democratic institutions less seriously, much of the shock value of someone like Kanye "Ye" West running a U.S. presidential campaign is lost.

The threshold for whom the public sees fit for public office has evolved, much like our media consumption habits have evolved and much like the discourse of politics has evolved. Treating electoral politics as sport primes voters to perceive politicians as celebrities and celebrities as politicians.

Celebrity candidates and candidate celebrities

Some belove actor Morgan Freeman for his iconic role in *Driving Miss Daisy*; others revere him for his roles in critically acclaimed films *The Shawshank Redemption* and the suspenseful *Seven*. Freeman established himself as a Hollywood heavyweight by playing wise, rational, and even-keeled characters. Do these traits sound like the traits of a strong presidential candidate? Well, about 81% of the public thinks so, according to a 2020 poll conducted by *The Daily Show* and YouGov. Pitting randomized hypothetical candidates against one another for survey participants, the poll found that a strong majority of Americans believe Freeman would make an effective president; Tom Hanks and Denzel Washington were runners up. Hanks' name resurfaced yet again when consumer marketing firm Piplsay released results of an online poll conducted in 2021. The firm found widespread public support for Hanks, Angelina Jolie, and Will Smith as potential presidential candidates. (It should be noted that data collection preceded the Oscar's slap between Smith and comedian Chris Rock.) The poll also found that 58% of respondents said they would vote for Dwayne "the Rock" Johnson or Matthew McConaughey – both of whom contemplated a run for Texas governor.

These polls underscore a trend among voters that suggest that the public is increasingly embracing entertainers as viable candidates. But what explains the sudden clamor for celebrity candidates? And how effective are they in winning elections?

One important factor in the growing acceptance for celebrity candidates is the increasing appeal for **outsider candidates**, meaning candidates who are not part of the Washington establishment and have never held elected office. A considerable number of high-profile "outsider" candidates have run for public office in recent years. Mark Kelly, a respected NASA astronaut, beat an incumbent in the 2020 special election for the vacant U.S. Senate seat in Arizona and won reelection in 2022. Pilot Amy McGrath ran for a U.S. Senate seat in Kentucky; neurosurgeon Ben Carson and entrepreneur Andrew Yang ran for president. A disengaged electorate, meaning an electorate less participatory and more cynical about the political system, is generally more attracted to outsider candidates. Research shows that candidates who frame themselves as outsiders are well received by voters, regardless of how little political experience they hold (Hansen & Treul, 2021). A 2018 poll conducted by Monmouth University showed that a majority of U.S. voters, 52%, indicated not merely that they would support an outsider congressional candidate but, in fact, preferred the outsiders (Sparks, 2019).

For voters, name recognition is an important criterion for a candidate, and this has celebrities particularly primed to run for office. First, the public more easily identifies celebrities than prominent political leaders and ranks celebrities higher in terms of favorability than political elites (Wright, 2020). Voters, regardless of their political ideology and level of campaign engagement, indicate a preference for supporting celebrity candidates over unknown candidates (Zwarun & Torrey, 2011). Ronald Reagan's charm was part of the bipartisan appeal for his gubernatorial and presidential campaigns, which underscores other advantages celebrity candidates tend to reap: the advantage not just of name recognition but of charisma and physical attractiveness (Samuels, 2021). These traits play an increasingly important role given the emphasis on image and visual communication in today's media environment.

Pandey (2021) notes that the increasing number of celebrity candidates also parallels the trend of celebrities interjecting themselves in politics more routinely, with high public endorsements and political statements (a trend explored in Chapter 5). Some scholars have observed a growing belief among the electorate that celebrities can fix a broken political system with as much ease as their on-screen characters solve problems in films (Babcock & Whitehouse, 2005). Just the same way that wily detective William Somerset can solve grisly murders in *Seven* perhaps Freeman can improve functionality of Washington that voters are feeling increasingly cynical about. Because of its proximity to Hollywood, this trust in celebrities over established politicians is especially prominent in California state politics.

Actor Ronald Reagan served two terms as president from 1981 to 1988, after a successful stint in state politics where he was elected governor of California from 1967 to 1975. Of course, the "terminator" – or "governator" – also served as the governor of California; actor Arnold Schwarzenegger was elected from 2003 to 2011 after playing iconic Hollywood action roles in films like *The Terminator* and *Total Recall*. On a local level, Clint Eastwood was elected mayor of Carmel-by-the-Sea in 1986. Singer and songwriter Sonny Bono was elected mayor of Palm Springs in 1988 and later to the U.S. House of Representatives. In 2008, Kevin Johnson, the three-time NBA all-star guard, easily defeated an incumbent to become mayor of Sacramento. Nonetheless, the power of name recognition can provide celebrities in any state with an electoral advantage.

President Trump isn't the only reality television star elected to public office. After appearing on MTV's *Real World: Boston* in 1998, Sean Duffy, a former prosecutor and sports commentator, was elected to four terms in the U.S. House of Representatives in Wisconsin. Immediately after retiring from the NBA in 1977, New York Knicks forward Bill Bradley launched a campaign for the U.S. Senate in New Jersey. (After serving three terms, the Democrat unsuccessfully ran for president in 2000). In 1998, WWF wrestler

Jesse "The Body" Ventura was narrowly elected governor of Minnesota as a third-party candidate. Ventura previously served as mayor of Brooklyn Park, Minnesota. And before Al Franken was elected to the U.S. Senate in 2009, the comedian was best known for his work on *Saturday Night Live*. Franken, a Democrat from Minnesota, narrowly defeated a Republican incumbent by just over 300 votes. (He was later pressured to resign by party elites in 2018, after news broke of sexual misconduct allegations). Despite the name recognition and on-camera comfort that benefits celebrity candidates, for every electoral success story, there are at least one or two unsuccessful campaigns.

For example, controversial radio shock jock Howard Stern ran an unsuccessful campaign for New York governor in 1994. Actress Cynthia Nixon, from *Sex and the City*, lost in a 2018 bid to unseat incumbent New York governor Andrew Cuomo. Actors Fred Thompson and Roseann Barr ran presidential campaigns that quickly fizzled in 2008 and 2012, respectively. Celebrities have also misfired on state-level seats and local elections. Actresses Stacey Dash and Melissa Gilbert couldn't capitalize on their celebrity status to win state-level elections. *American Idol*'s Clay Aiken also fell short in his efforts to unseat a Republican incumbent for a North Carolina U.S. Senate seat after narrowly winning the primary contest (and he also ran unsuccessfully for a House seat in 2022). Childhood star Ben Savage was unsuccessful in his campaign to land a seat on the West Hollywood City Council, totaling just 7% of votes. Nonetheless, in March 2023, Savage announced via Instagram the launch of his campaign for U.S. House of Representatives. Despite just as many electoral failures as victories for celebrity candidates, it has not stopped some from exploiting celebrity status as part of their campaign strategy.

Chances are you have not heard of the show, *Jeg Er Ambassadøren fra Amerika*, let alone can pronounce it. The Netflix show translates to *I Am the Ambassador From America* in English and featured Rufus Gifford. After President Obama appointed the former Hollywood producer as ambassador to Denmark in 2013, Gifford authored cookbooks and a best-selling biography. The publications, along with his popular reality television show, put his entire life on display for the Danish people. While serving in a diplomatic position that was traditionally shrouded in some degree of privacy, Gifford cultivated a celebrity persona – a strategy that may ultimately broaden his political career. In a news interview, Gifford told reporters that the goals of the reality show were to "humanize" government and make it "sexier" (Vice News, 2016). He continued in saying that he wanted to distinguish his program from the Kardashian "brand" of reality TV. Use of the word "brand" here is quite telling. The brand he built through reality television rendered Gifford a star in Denmark. The Danish people mounted a campaign encouraging him to run for U.S. president and band Lukas Graham dedicated its song "Nice Guy" to Gifford at a music festival in 2016 (Weiss-Meyer, 2016). Nonetheless, celebrity status and diplomacy experience do not guarantee electoral success. Gifford announced on Twitter in 2017 that he would run for a seat in the U.S. House of Representatives in Massachusetts but ultimately finished fifth in the primary.

Celebrity candidates typically follow one of two trajectories into politics. Ronald Reagan eased his way into politics. First, he took a political position as the president of the Screen Actors Guild and was later elected governor of California in 1966. The two-term president embraced some state and local experience before advancing to the national political arena. But the notion of celebrity candidates with zero experience in public office is increasingly prevalent in today's age of abundant media and widespread distrust of political institutions (Pandey, 2021). First, the world saw the success of reality television star, and Twitter afficionado Donald Trump elected U.S. president in 2016. In that same year, television comedian Jimmy Morales was elected the president of Guatemala, and although the focus of this text is U.S. campaigns, we could look at Ukraine president Volodymyr Zelenskyy if we wanted to really get meta. The comedic actor played the role of *president* in a popular television series *Servant of the People* from 2015 to 2019. Without any political experience, he fashioned himself as an anti-establishment outsider, winning handedly in 2019 and assuming the highest office in Ukraine. This trend of celebrity candidates without political experience making inroads resurfaced again in the USA in the 2020 and 2022 elections.

Before rapper Kanye West was making headlines for anti-Semitic remarks, "Ye" was making headlines for an unexpected run at the White House in 2020. West launched his campaign just four months before the presidential election. With zero experience in public office, the rapper pulled less than 1% of the vote but nonetheless announced his intentions to run again in 2024. Democrat Marianne Williamson, an author and self-help guru did not fare much better in the 2020 primaries. With her lack of political experience especially clear during the debates, Williamson was the center of several viral memes and late-night television punchlines but has nonetheless launched her 2024 presidential campaign. In a California special election in effort to recall Governor Gavin Newsom, Caitlyn Jenner, former Olympian and transgender activist, ran in 2021. Without any political experience, the Republican pulled just 1% of the votes. Although celebrities without political experience are no shoo-in for electoral success, voters are seeing more celebrities on ballots in recent elections and close races in the 2022 midterms suggest a "normalizing" of outsider celebrity candidates without political experience.

In Arizona, local celebrity news anchor Kari Lake was nearly elected governor in 2022. Despite lacking any political experience and a campaign dogged by controversial statements including the denial of the 2020 U.S. presidential election results, Lake pulled 49.6% of the vote in the general election. Known for his medical expertise on *The Oprah Winfrey Show* and *The Dr. Oz Show*, Dr. Mehmet Oz was the Republican nominee in a high-profile U.S. Senate race in Pennsylvania. The physician, author, and political outsider came close to winning the critical seat (although the tightening of the race was partly attributed to the stroke his Democratic opponent, John Fetterman, suffered a few months before the election). Another celebrity lacking political experience also turned heads in 2022 when he forced incumbent Raphael Warnock, a respected reverend, to a run-off election in Georgia. Hall of Fame football player and Heisman Trophy winner Herschel Walker garnered 48.7% of the general election runoff despite zero political experience and a slew of domestic violence allegations. These races suggest that voters are warming up to celebrities without political experience and see them as viable candidates. The vote shares, despite the losses, suggest that well-known political novices are inching closer to electoral success.

The role of celebrity in electoral politics manifests in other ways beyond the celebrity candidate. Some politicians have looked to carve out celebrity status after serving in public office. Former Cincinnati city councilor and mayor Jerry Springer moved on to become a talk show host after his stint in public office. *The Jerry Springer Show* aired for nearly 20 years, creating a blueprint for the trashy daytime talk format. After representing Tennessee in the U.S. Senate, Fred Thompson refined his acting chops to play a judge on *Law & Order*. And after being punched into John McCain's 2008 ticket, former governor Sarah Palin sought the limelight a little longer by hosting reality television program *Sarah Palin's Alaska*. And even ordinary members of the electorate may emerge as pseudo-celebrities in today's contemporary campaign environment, where enough chatter on social media lands anyone a sliver of spotlight.

Aspiring model Amber Lee Ettinger, or "Obama girl," achieved fame for appearing in the viral video "Crush on Obama" after it was posted to YouTube in 2007. Ettinger became the subject of cable news segments and appeared on *Saturday Night Live* following the video's release. In that same election year, Samuel Joseph Wurzelbacher became a middle-class superhero of sorts when he asked Obama a question about the implications of his tax policies on small businesses. Wurzelbacher, who planned to open a plumbing business, was routinely referenced as "Joe the Plumber" by the McCain-Palin campaign as a nod to the everyday American. (Interestingly, Wurzelbacher attempted to capitalize on that fame by running for a U.S. House of Representatives seat in Ohio in 2012 but ultimately lost to the incumbent.) And Ken Bone, a powerplant operator from Illinois, attracted a cult following online after asking a thoughtful energy-related question during the town hall debate in the 2016 presidential election. He became beloved for his low-key civility in an otherwise-hostile campaign, and for the infamous red cardigan, he wore on live television. Bone now operates a verified Twitter account with more than 146,000 followers.

Entertainment and politics are so intertwined in media's long-tail environment that social media and mainstream media work in tandem to speculate about celebrity candidates before they even seek elected office. News reports generated stories about the possibility of Mark Cuban, star of reality television show *Shark Tank* and owner of the Dallas Mavericks, running for president in 2016, 2020, and 2024. Of course, the news media was also preoccupied with the prospect of another celebrity in the White House in 2020, after Oprah Winfrey made a well-received speech at the 2018 Golden Globe Awards. Although Winfrey made no public indication that she was considering public office, the idea of an Oprah presidential campaign generated social media buzz and countless news headlines including headlines for *The Guardian, People, The Huffington Post, Politico, 60 Minutes, PBS, CNN, The Washington Post, CBS,* and *The Hill.*

Whether it's the public warming up to celebrity candidates, regardless of political experience, the increasing frequency in which celebrities run for office (or ruminate a run for office), or media hype for celebrities that have not formally launched a campaign, celebrity has achieved a new level of clout in the electoral process. But no celebrity – or politician – can expand their brand without merchandise and a burgeoning fanbase. Here's how some political candidates are continuing to commercialize their campaigns through marketing and merch.

Show me that swag! Campaign fandom and merch

Next time you're stopped at an intersection, look at the vehicles you see. It doesn't have to be an election year to see evidence of campaign branding. Perhaps you see an American-made pickup with oversized tires and a Trump 2024 flag undulating from the back of the truck bed. Or you spot a sporty, hybrid crossover cluttered with such an abundance of Hillary Clinton, HRC (Human Rights Campaign), and national park stickers you can barely make out the color of the car. Imagine you're at a packed outdoor event in rural America. A decorative mobile truck sets up shop and unrolls its windows, unveiling T-shirts, posters, and hats galore. But this isn't Coachella, and these shirts aren't donning the names of Bad Bunny, Frank Ocean, or other artists working the festival circuit. These shirts are printed with "Boot. Edge. Edge" and this mobile merch station is selling gear from Democratic candidate Pete Buttigieg – not festival headliners. You no longer must imagine this scenario; it's already reality.

Merchandise is not a completely new byproduct of the modern campaign era, but campaign goods have evolved considerably from lawn signs and bumper stickers. The marketing gimmicks of today's campaigns include branded baby onesies, hoodies, dolls, and flasks. The merch is married with informal slogans, contests, and giveaways to create a multipronged marketing campaign that feels more aligned with rockstars, athletes, and entertainers than stiff suits seeking elected office. Today's campaign environment requires not only that candidates adopt many of the marketing strategies of the entertainment world but also that they do so with increasing creativity.

Branding plays a critical role in the modern campaign. First, the selling of merchandise boosts campaign fundraising. With most goods ranging between $20 and $100, the purchases reduce the overall individual campaign donation averages for candidates and contest giveaways also ensure an outpouring of small donations. Buttigieg's campaign even organized a contest prize for the supporter who contributed the *lowest* donation. Small donations help candidates craft a **populist** public persona, meaning that they appear to understand the plight and challenges that everyday Americans face. Both Democratic candidates Bernie Sanders and Elizabeth Warren would often point to the low dollar averages of individual campaign contributions received to reinforce themselves as populist candidates that aren't beholden to big donors and corporate interests. The online sales of merch and contest giveaways provide candidates a way to raise money without seeming too elite or backed by the uberwealthy.

Of course, campaigns still sell the conventional merchandise – bumper stickers, lawn signs, and coffee mugs – but during the 2016 presidential election, Trump took "the art of the deal" to new heights. His campaign's red Make America Great Again hat, or MAGA hat, became an iconic symbol of candidate branding and the last two presidential election cycles have seen the floodgates of creative candidate merchandising open. In 2016, Clinton's campaign sold barbeque grilling aprons, and Jeb Bush's campaign sold unusual items from branded flasks to guacamole bowls. In 2020, the Sanders' campaign sold pocket-sized "Bernie" dolls, and Kanye's campaign sold hoodies for $160. That year also saw Amy Klobuchar's campaign sell tea towels and linens. More recently, Trump – running for president in 2024 – made an appearance in East Palestine, Ohio, following a catastrophic train derailment and chemical spill. He used the visit to hand out Trump branded bottled water and his signature MAGA hats (McDougall, 2023). Ye has reportedly stockpiled merchandise from brands that severed ties with him following anti-Semitic remarks and plans to resell Adidas apparel with his "Ye2024" logo (Saul, 2022). And the 2024 presidential campaign for Ron DeSantis sold $35 T-shirts reading "stop pussyfooting around" just hours after he lodged the soundbite as an attack on California Governor Gavin Newsom, referencing his preoccupation with Florida and presidential politics.

Giveaways too have evolved. Obama offered dinner contests during his 2008 campaign, but candidates raised the stakes by 2020. Cory Booker offered supporters the chance to win an all-expenses paid dinner not only with him but also with his actress girlfriend Rosario Dawson, according to his contest Twitter announcement. Not to be outdone, Buttigieg's campaign included the opportunity for donors to win trips to his hometown and an all-paid trip for two to see *Hamilton* in San Francisco with Buttigieg's husband. Perhaps no giveaway was as appealing or newsy as Democrat John Delaney's donor contest for winning a trip for two to Washington, D.C., to accompany the candidate to Game 4 of the World Series.

The merch can also serve as a campaign strategy for advancing policy positions and communicating values. The MAGA hat signaled conservative values and Trump's branded plastic straws tapped into Republican outrage over climate change policies. Marjorie Taylor Greene, a Republican member of the U.S. House of Representatives seeking reelection in 2022, sold hats and shirts labeled "Defund the FBI" on her campaign website to stir public outrage over the bureau's search of Trump's Mar-a-Lago property. Greene, who isn't afraid of controversy, previously sold "Proud Christian Nationalist" gear during her reelection campaign. Democratic presidential candidate Andrew Yang released a series of shirts and hats that featured a marijuana leaf and the word MATH in capitalized letters. The clothing reinforced candidate support for the legalization of marijuana. Elizabeth Warren's 2020 campaign onesies also served as a reminder to voters about where she stood on policy issues such as paid family leave. Today's merch not only helps campaigns fundraise but also communicates values and policies associated with that candidate. Others use branded products to demonstrate humor and authenticity to voters.

Presidential campaign merchandise can also reinforce character narratives about the candidates and play up likable aspects of their public image. Minnesota native Amy Klobuchar embraced her folksy Midwestern charm with merchandise that included family recipes and branded ice scrapers. Buttigieg capitalized on the difficulty the average voter had in pronouncing his name. His campaign released phonetically spelled T-shirts that read "Boot. Edge. Edge." The Biden campaign sold gear featuring the candidate wearing his iconic Aviator sunglasses; Clinton's campaign included branded pant suit T-shirts. The Sanders' campaign reinforced the narrative of his cranky uncle persona, selling apparel that read "Uncle Bernie" and "Tio Bernie" – with some shirts featuring the oversized, and now internet famous, mittens the Vermont Senator wore. And Marco Rubio's 2016 campaign communicated light-hearted humor to voters when it sold exclusive "Marco Polo" polo shirts for $45.

The more creative and novel campaigns are with their merchandise and giveaways, the more online buzz and mainstream news attention they attract. Slogans can help market the candidates and generate media attention, too. "Feel the Bern" and "Yang Gang" became not only heavily used catchphrases by supporters but also the subject of campaign merch and social media hashtags for the Sanders and Yang campaigns.

Campaign merch can be unifying or confrontational but operates as an indirect way for showing dissatisfaction or pride with the direction of the country. More directly, it's a way for people to signal their political fandom, much like we continue to wear gear for our favorite sports team even during the off season or when they fail to reach the playoffs. The electorate's proud display of campaign merchandise conceptualizes the supporters as "fans" of a political party or candidate. If the electorate is the fans, then that makes the politicians the celebrity "athletes" and their political parties or campaigns the "teams." And these conceptualizations only contribute to the increasing commoditization of the contemporary campaign.

Summary

The blurring of entertainment and politics manifests in many ways. First, we've seen heightened emphasis on spectacle from the news media covering political campaigns. The rhetoric from both the news media and public officials has shifted as people across political institutions more routinely use sports jargon, treating politics as competitive sport rather than serious governing. This desire to keep elections entertaining may not only be necessary to keep low-information voters in the fold but also leave the electorate often feeling more cynical about politics and political institutions.

The last few election cycles have seen a spike in celebrity candidates, particularly celebrity outsiders with little experience in governance or policymaking. Moreover, the public is taking these candidates more seriously and the media quickly join in speculating celebrity candidacies and amplifying their viability. Merchandise and giveaways are becoming a greater part of campaign strategy, as campaigns deploy consumer marketing strategies to brand candidates and attract media attention. These developments rewire how we think about politics, prompting us to experience campaigns through the lens of sport, celebrity, and fandom. These trends help us understand why contemporary campaigns are being run through entertainment media. The following chapters will unpack innovative ways candidates strategically navigate this shift in campaign norms.

Resources and references

Associated Press. (2007, July 15). Bush runs White House with sports metaphors. *NBC News*. www.nbcnews.com/id/wbna19774480

Babcock, W., & Whitehouse, V. (2005). Celebrity as a postmodern phenomenon, electoral crisis for democracy, and media nightmare. *Journal of Mass Media Ethics*, *20*(2–3), 176–191.

Belt, T. L., Just, M. R., & Crigler, A. N. (2012). The 2008 media primary: Handicapping the candidates in newspapers, on TV, cable, and the internet. *The International Journal of Press/Politics*, *17*(3), 341–369.

Brenan, M. (2021, October 7). Americans' trust in media dips to second lowest on record. *Gallup*. https://news.gallup.com/poll/355526/americans-trust-media-dips-second-lowest-record.aspx

Butterworth, M. L. (2014). Nate silver and campaign 2012: Sport, the statistical frame, and the rhetoric of electoral forecasting. *Journal of Communication*, *64*(5), 895–914.

The Daily Show. (2020, August 19). The Daily Show/YouGov: Who do Americans want as their next celebrity president? *YouGov America*. https://today.yougov.com/topics/entertainment/articles-reports/2020/08/19/daily-show-yougov-celebrity-president-poll

Decker, C. (2013, November 15). Obama's sports metaphors: Obamacare as slippery as football. *Los Angeles Times*. www.latimes.com/politics/la-xpm-2013-nov-15-la-pn-obamacare-obama-football-golf-20131115-story.html

Dunaway, J. (2008). Markets, ownership, and the quality of campaign news coverage. *The Journal of Politics*, *70*(4), 1193–1202.

Farnsworth, S. J., & Lichter, S. R. (2011). *The nightly news nightmare: Media coverage of U.S. presidential elections, 1988–2008*. Rowman & Littlefield.

Hamilton, J. T. (2004). *All the news that's fit to sell: How the market transforms information into news*. Princeton University Press.

Hansen, E. R., & Treul, S. A. (2021). Inexperienced vs. anti-establishment: Voter preferences for outsider congressional candidates. *Research & Politics, 8*(3). https://doi.org/10.1177/20531680211034958

Iyengar, S., Norpoth, H., & Hahn, K. S. (2004). Consumer demand for election news: The horserace sells. *The Journal of Politics, 66*(1), 157–175.

Lawrence, R. G. (2000). Game-framing the issues: Tracking the strategy frame in public policy news. *Political Communication, 17*(2), 93–114.

Mann, R. (2016, April 2013). How the "Daisy" ad changed everything about political advertising. *Smithsonian Magazine.* www.smithsonianmag.com/history/how-daisy-ad-changed-everything-about-political-advertising-180958741/

Martinez, S. (2015, August 6). *Is sports lingo in politics ruining the game?* [Video]. Newsy. www.newsy.com/stories/is-sports-lingo-in-politics-ruining-the-game/

McDougall, A. J. (2023, February 22). Trump brings Trump-branded water to Ohio residents after train derailment. *The Daily Beast.* www.thedailybeast.com/donald-trump-hawks-trump-water-in-east-palestine-after-train-derailment

Moran, K. (2019, July 31). CNN's movie trailer-style debate intro was too much for some people to handle. *The Huffington Post.* www.huffpost.com/entry/cnn-democratic-debate-intro_n_5d414a2ee4b01d8c97838ffd

Pandey, E. (2021, October 19). Celebrities are America's new politicians. *Axios.* www.axios.com/2021/10/19/celebrity-political-candidates-matthew-mcconaughey-caitlyn-jenner

Patterson, T. (2016, December 7). *News coverage of the 2016 general election: How the press failed the voters.* Shorenstein Center on Media, Politics and Public Policy. https://shorensteincenter.org/news-coverage-2016-general-election/

Pew. (2022, June 6). *Public trust in government: 1958–2022.* Pew Research Center. www.pewresearch.org/politics/2022/06/06/public-trust-in-government-1958-2022/

Samuels, A. (2021, April 9). Why Americans can't resist a celebrity political candidate. *FiveThirtyEight.* https://fivethirtyeight.com/features/why-americans-cant-resist-a-celebrity-political-candidate/

Saul, D. (2022, November 21). Kanye West says he'll sell his Adidas and Balenciaga merch with "Ye2024" presidential campaign logo for $20. *Forbes.* www.forbes.com/sites/dereksaul/2022/11/21/kanye-west-says-hell-sell-his-adidas-and-balenciaga-merch-with-ye2024-presidential-campaign-logo-for-20/?sh=733e1f466962

Sigelman, L., & Bullock, D. (2016). Candidates, issues, horse races, and hoopla: Presidential campaign coverage, 1888–1988. *American Politics Research, 19*(1), 5–32.

Sparks, G. (2019, February 14). Do Americans really want outsider politicians? *CNN.* www.cnn.com/2019/02/14/politics/political-outsiders/index.html

Stevenson, A. (1956). *Address accepting the presidential nomination at the democratic national convention in Chicago.* The American Presidency Project. www.presidency.ucsb.edu/documents/address-accepting-the-presidential-nomination-the-democratic-national-convention-chicago

Thorson, E. A., & Serazio, M. (2018). Sports fandom and political attitudes. *Public Opinion Quarterly, 82*(2), 391–403.

Turcotte, J. (2017). Predicting policy: Exploring news attention to policy issues in electoral debates. *Journal of Applied Communication Research, 45*(5), 576–595.

Vallone, R., Less, R., & Lepper, M. (1985). The hostile media phenomenon: Biased perception and perceptions of media bias in coverage of the Beirut massacre. *Journal of Personality and Social Psychology, 49*, 577–588.

Vice News. (2016, November 16). *The U.S. ambassador is treated like a rockstar in Denmark* [Video]. YouTube. www.youtube.com/watch?v=LbkmJsGv8cg

Vox. (2017, April 17). *CNN treats politics like sports – and it's making us all dumber* [Video]. YouTube. www.youtube.com/watch?v=4pS4x8hXQ5c

Washington Post Staff. (2020, February 28). Merch madness: The presidential campaigns' battle over branding. *The Washington Post*. www.washingtonpost.com/graphics/2020/politics/2020-campaign-merchandise-candidate-strategy/

Weiss-Meyer, A. (2016, October). Big in Denmark: The U.S. ambassador. *The Atlantic*. www.theatlantic.com/magazine/archive/2016/10/denmark/497543/

Wright, L. (2020). *Star power: American democracy in the age of the celebrity candidate*. Routledge.

Zwarun, L., & Torrey, A. (2011). Somebody versus nobody: An exploration of the role of celebrity status in an election. *The Social Science Journal, 48*(4), 672–680.

3 From daytime talk to late-night punchlines

Campaign strategy and soft news

"He's got lots of experience down South. Came from Texas, where everything is bigger. Turned Florida from a limp peninsula to a virile member of the U.S. economy," Jimmy Fallon whispered soothingly on-air on June 16, 2015, as he introduced the latest collaborator in his "slow jam the news segment" on *Tonight With Jimmy Fallon*. This introduction shortly followed Jeb Bush's lines acknowledging that he thought "long and hard" about running for president. Yes, this was the same Jeb Bush from the prominent Republican family, son and brother to two former presidents and the early favorite among evangelical Christian voters in the 2016 presidential election. It is difficult to imagine presidents Kennedy, Nixon, or Bush, Sr. engaging with media in this way – and with good reason.

When Kennedy appeared on *Tonight Starring Jack Paar* in 1960, it marked the first time a presidential candidate visited a late-night television program. His challenger, Republican Richard Nixon, quickly followed suit. Despite being in the domain of entertainment television, the segments largely conformed to the conventions of presidential politics with both appearances remaining serious in tone with little comedic value. Nonetheless, critics and columnists lambasted the candidates for their late-night-television appearances. *New York Times* columnist James Reston felt it undermined democracy and argued that candidates proving how relaxed they could be on late-night television was "diminishing intellectual capacity" of U.S. voters (Andrews, 2016). The critiques captured what would be an uneasy relationship between presidential politics and entertainment television that would persist for decades. Such appearances from candidates were infrequent and overly serious in tone, but campaigns are often molded by the media of their time. Sooner or later, candidates, willingly or begrudgingly, must learn to adapt to the media preferences of the electorate.

Kennedy, routinely described as the first television president, embraced the medium of his time and took risks in expanding the conventions of the modern presidential campaign by gazing into a teleprompter. Those risks paid off for Kennedy in the 1960 election. Nevertheless, campaign engagement with television in the following decades remained mostly confined to news programming. Yet television is an entertaining medium – and the distinction between news and

DOI: 10.4324/9781003364832-3

entertainment began to erode in the 1980s, with cable television reaching a critical mass. The entertaining cable options signaled heightened influence of soft news in political campaign communication. **Soft news** is typically defined as programs that while informative or personally useful have a primary purpose of entertaining its audience. Another term often used to describe soft news programs is "infotainment," meaning the combined content of information and entertainment.

Although network television has lost some of its influence in today's era of media abundance, the relevancy of soft news programs has persisted in large part due to their agenda-setting effects. These programs continue to generate headlines across mainstream news media and candid moments on talk-formatted programs are also amplified across social media platforms. This chapter explores the strategic use of soft news programs – specifically daytime talk shows and late-night television – and how candidates use these platforms to introduce themselves to the American public, connect with more tailored segments of the electorate, and relate to voters.

The couch as a campaign stump

Daytime talk shows were historically perceived as venues for matriarchs of the household interested in family and domestic issues, celebrities, and pop culture (i.e., *The Oprah Winfrey Show* or *The Phil Donohue Show*). Or they were seen as a place devoid of civility, a place where hosts would reveal the father of babies through a dramatic paternity test or invite past enemies of a guest to come to the set to bury the hatchet – or, better yet, throw one (i.e., *The Jerry Springer Show* or *The Jenny Jones Show*). Rarely were they thought of as a venue for serious political discourse or a serious campaign stop for political candidates. What changed that? The better question would be *who* changed that.

National news figure and ABC journalist Barbara Walters introduced a new format that combined a more informational, newsy approach to the structure of daytime talk. *The View* premiered in 1997, featuring four – though soon to be five – women of diverse backgrounds and perspectives engaging in banter centered on the issues of the day. Journalist Amanda FitzSimons (2019) noted that the appeal of *The View* can be attributed to the authenticity of the hosts and the show's apolitical premise or, as she has described, a political talk show that isn't perceived as a political talk show. The conversations among the hosts are often intimate and raw, the hosts reveal just as much about themselves as their guests do, and the discourse reflects the complicated and emotional political climate we live in. Early seasons of the program featured an array of political guests but Barack Obama's 2010 appearance, which marked only the second time a sitting president appeared on a daytime talk program, helped bolster the show's news chops.

Obama's appearance came just a few months ahead of the midterm elections at a time when the fiscally conservative Tea Party emerged as a vocal critic of his administration and as a movement within the Republican Party that was poised to flip some Congressional seats held by Democrats. The interview provided the president with an opportunity to balance the personal with the political. He spoke about family traditions and a recent vacation to Maine. Importantly, the interview was an opportunity for him to address the war in Afghanistan and highlight economic recovery from the 2007 housing crisis that unfolded just before his first term. The president received a warm reception from an energetic studio audience, and the strategic move shattered expectations for how a sitting president could – and *should* – engage with entertainment media. Ten years before a sitting president took notice, political candidates were slowly reshaping campaign expectations with visits on daytime talk programs.

Despite Oprah Winfrey's influence as the Emmy-award winning "queen" of daytime talk, the host largely avoided interviewing political figures. It wasn't until 2000, 14 years on air, when Oprah hosted her first presidential candidate; she interviewed both Al Gore and George W. Bush (see **Case Study 3.1**). According to political communication scholar Matthew Baum (2005), the 2000 campaign marked a turning point for strategic use of soft news, with presidential candidates making appearances on not just the late-night television circuit but also daytime talk: *Oprah, Live! With Regis,* and *The Rosie O'Donnell Show* all welcomed candidates that year. Despite Clinton's success following his iconic *Arsenio Hall Show* visit in 1992, daytime television remained overlooked by most campaigns for years but 2000 was different for a few reasons.

Case Study 3.1   George W. Bush charms Oprah and studio audience

Figure 3.1 George W. Bush greets Oprah Winfrey as he settles in for an hour-long interview.

Source: Illustration by Eduardo Rangel.

On September 19, 2000, six weeks ahead of the U.S. presidential election and one week following Democratic opponent Al Gore's interview on the program, George W. Bush showcased his capacity to deliver **political narratives** or storytelling that can shape public discourse around an issue, campaign, or candidate, as he settled in on a couch opposite Oprah Winfrey. The hour-long interview allowed his humility, values, and humor to shine. His narratives included an emotional story about his wife's health scares during the pregnancy of their twin daughters and the challenges the couple faced regarding infertility. The struggles were relatable and showed the candidate as a compassionate man who reflects on faith and family. Bush also shared a light-hearted story about meeting Queen Elizabeth II as a child. After an exchange with his grandmother, the Queen asked if he was the "black sheep" of the family; he responded by asking her if she had any [black sheep] in her family. The audience erupted in laughter and the moment captured his sense of humor and accentuated his relatability. Even his blunders seemed to work in his favor and humanize the candidate. During Oprah's "favorite things" segment, Bush mistakenly attributed his favorite song "Wake up Little Susie" to Buddy Holly rather than The Everly Brothers. He seized the interview as an opportunity to dispel the myth that he was simply running on his father's name and assuaged voter fears that his presidency would be an extension of his father's. His quips and folksy banter highlighted the charm of a candidate that doesn't take themselves too seriously and a departure from the public persona of George H. W. Bush, who left office with a low approval rating and a reputation as a stoic conservative out of touch with the average American. This was George W.'s campaign now. He embraced the **gaffes**, political blunders or missteps that cause embarrassment or criticism; Bush's missteps helped to build his "plain folks" appeal. Bush successfully exuded the qualities lacking in his father, building credibility with voters one quip and smile at a time. George W. Bush was now his own man, free from the burdens and assumptions that came with carrying the Bush family name. He was campaigning as the candidate who could relate to anyone. The Bush campaign referred to his penchant for relatability as "compassionate conservatism" – and this warmer brand of Republicanism was effectively on display in his interview with Oprah.

First, the fragmentation of news audiences had accelerated considerably by 2000, with websites and blogs chipping away at the mass audiences of mainstream media outlets. Widespread household adoption of the internet provided the public with new outlets for entertainment. According to Pew (2021),

2000 marked the first time that internet access eclipsed 50% of U.S. homes. While cable television, with its abundance of entertaining channels, may have wet the public's appetite for entertainment media, the web dramatically intensified the craving. Second, the 2000 campaign came after the launch of Walters' *The View*, meaning that the media environment was already being shaped by a melding of news and entertainment, with both late-night television and daytime talk emerging as prominent platforms for political discourse during a time when the electorate was becoming less attentive to traditional news media. Finally, the 2000 U.S. presidential election featured two young nominees willing to take some campaign risks: Gore, 52, and Bush, 54. After their inclusion of daytime talk in their 2000 campaigns, the talk show format became a necessary campaign stump, regardless of candidate age, party affiliation, and level of name recognition.

Trump appeared numerous times on *The View* before he was elected president, and some pundits have suggested that Hillary Clinton's lone visit on *The View* was not enough in the 2016 election and that the campaign didn't make its candidate accessible enough to the talk show circuit. But Clinton did appear on *Ellen*, where she addressed the double standard of women in politics and issues relating to women's rights. Clinton also engaged in political narratives. She shared the story of being denied a credit card by a bank in 1976, noting that the bank told her she would need to use her husband's card. She quickly pointed out to the audience that she made more money than her husband. Clinton drew many moments of applause, and although the interview may not have humanized her to a broad audience, the campaign stop likely reinforced support with those receptive to her candidacy. Audience reactions for soft news can be a revealing tool for any campaign.

Beto O'Rourke, the Democratic congressman from Texas, used the Oprah Winfrey Network as a testing ground to gauge public enthusiasm for his presidential candidacy. The unofficial candidate appeared in an interview with Oprah in February 2019, to drop that he is "thinking about running for president." The statement prompted roaring cheers from the audience and probing follow-up questions from Oprah to determine whether O'Rourke was making his candidacy official in that moment. The warm reception was a thumbs up for O'Rourke to test the presidential waters. One month later, he officially launched his campaign. Daytime talk programs, with an audience that skews more apolitical and moderate than news audiences, can act as an unofficial litmus test to help campaigns measure public enthusiasm for candidates or policies with the live studio audience essentially exhibiting the characteristics of an informal focus group. Daytime talk also provides a forum for a first formal candidate introduction to a national audience.

During the 2020 election, Democratic Senator Cory Booker, of New Jersey, strategically planned an interview on *The View* on the same day that he announced the launch of his presidential campaign. Several campaigns were utilizing the same soft news playbook. Julian Castro, secretary of Housing and

Urban Development under Obama, followed the announcement of his campaign launch with an appearance on *The View*. Ohio Democrat Tim Ryan took it a step further by delivering his campaign announcement live on-air during *The View*, later acknowledging that the campaign hoped to reach moderate or Republican women who had reservations about President Trump (FitzSimons, 2019). Although President Biden did not make his 2020 campaign announcement on *The View*, his April 26, 2019, appearance on the show marked the first media interview he granted once making his official announcement the day prior. In other words, Biden followed up his campaign launch not with a scheduled sit-down with a reputable news organization but with a daytime talk program.

By 2014, no daytime television program had welcomed as many political candidates as *The View* and the show aired more than 25 interviews with presidential candidates by 2020 (Parkin, 2014; FitzSimons, 2019). *The View* hasn't shown any signs of slowing down. According to Nielsen, the data analytics firm that measures market and audience trends in television, the show remained the most watched daytime talk program from 2020 to 2022, attracting more than 2.4 million viewers (Wagmeister, 2022). Further expanding the program's political influence, *The View* recently added Republican strategist Ana Navarro as one of its permanent hosts, and other daytime talk shows are beginning to feature women from prominent political families, campaign strategists, and former candidates. Meghan McCain, daughter of the late Arizona Senator John McCain, provided a moderate Republican perspective on *The View*. The ABC program lured her away from *Outnumbered*, a daytime program on Fox News, to cohost from 2017 to 2021. The program has also featured Abby Huntsman, daughter of former Utah Governor Jon Huntsman, in the role of co-host. More recently, former presidential candidate and Hewlett-Packard CEO Carly Fiorina co-hosted a 2021 episode of *The View*. And NBC's *The Today Show* welcomed co-host Jenna Bush, daughter of George W. Bush, following Kathie Lee Gifford's exit in 2019.

A diverse and unabashedly outspoken group of hosts with varying life experiences and opinions allows *The View* to unpack serious issues with as much ease as it unpacks the lighter slices of pop culture. The talk format carefully melds entertainment with serious political matters – an infotainment trend that piqued a bit earlier in late-night television, perhaps because the domain and audience were seen as more male-dominated than the viewing audience for daytime talk. In the late-night format, candidates also learn to strike the right balance between the personal and the political, but under one additional constraint: the ability to take punchlines in stride and dish out some laughs.

Rolling with the punches – or punchlines

When Vice President Gerald Ford appeared on *The Dick Cavett Show* in 1974, the tenor was somber and serious. The subject matter, however personal, remained heavy. Ford's political narratives focused on his adolescent years, discussing openly his name change and the experience of indirect learning that he was adopted. The television appearance was more centered on the personal than policy but did little to demonstrate relatability to voters. Ford maintained a serious disposition throughout the interview. A year later, when Ronald Reagan – a two-term governor from California – appeared on *The Tonight Show Starring Johnny Carson*, seen as a more playful alternative to Cavett's program, he muted the Hollywood charm and charisma that would later be associated with his presidential terms. This was not Reagan the showman sitting across from the energetic Carson. Reagan used the appearance as a platform to establish his vision for small government, drawing attention to government waste. Reagan had moments of wit but maintained a policy-driven discussion without many deviations about his personal life. Both candidates, who would soon face each other in the 1976 Republican primaries, leveraged entertainment media to cement name recognition before a national audience but did so in ways that were in step with the traditional expectations of a president and presidential campaigns.

It would have been a stretch of the imagination to think about a candidate delivering a sexualized slow jam of the news or singing a self-authored song about their dog (as Republican presidential candidate Carly Fiorina did in 2016) during those campaigns of the 1970s, because engaging in such entertaining and "low brow" late-night television programs was seen as politically risky, as something that could undermine the office or cue the public to take the candidate less seriously. Thus, Reagan and Ford applied presidential decorum to the entertainment space rather than adapting to the conventions of the program. But in the contemporary campaign environment, Bush's "slow jammed" moment is not an anomaly, nor is it especially risky. In fact, many strategists today would call those moments campaign imperatives.

A bevy of other politicians have performed with Fallon to "slow jam" the news, including President Obama, Massachusetts Governor Mitt Romney, New Jersey Governor Chris Christie and, more recently, Pete Buttigieg, Bernie Sanders, and Kamala Harris. These segments are policy-focused, awkward, and comical – and equipped with deadpan delivery, lackluster vocals, sexual innuendo, and jabs at opponents. What they are not is serious. The segment represents a far cry from the earliest late-night television appearances from politicians and symbolizes a significant evolution in campaign strategy. In the arena of presidential politics, a longstanding belief that candidates should be serious began to fracture. But what shook up this tacitly followed code of campaign decorum? A pair of sunglasses and a saxophone.

Arkansas Governor Bill Clinton emerged on *The Arsenio Hall Show* in 1992 with all the pomp and circumstance of a rock star but without the name recognition. The lesser-known challenger would threaten to thwart George H. W. Bush from a second term by building a coalition of young voters and Black voters, and the 45-year-old candidate built those coalitions through entertainment media – be damned what the critics and pundits would say. Columnist George

Will and television journalist Barbara Walters scoffed at Clinton's bluesy introduction on the program where he donned a pair of sunglasses and performed an Elvis classic on the saxophone. Bush's press secretary dubbed Clinton a "John Belushi wannabe" (Andrews, 2016). But the unorthodox television appearance (**see Case Study 3.2**) paid off at the voting booth and provided candidates with a blueprint on how to navigate entertainment media.

Case Study 3.2   Clinton's entertaining *Arsenio Hall* appearance

Figure 3.2 Bill Clinton makes some noise when he strolls onto *The Arsenio Hall Show* playing the saxophone.

Source: Illustration by Eduardo Rangel.

On June 3, 1992, Arkansas Governor Bill Clinton emerged on *The Arsenio Hall Show* stage with a saxophone and sunglasses, belting out *Heart Break Hotel* on the woodwind instrument. Clinton's bluesy introduction to the national political arena came with considerable fanfare and criticism, but with this unusual interview with Hall, the first Black late-night television host, Clinton made considerable inroads with Black voters. The appearance coincided with a tumultuous time, weeks after the L. A. riots. During the program, taped at Paragon Studios in Los Angeles, Clinton shared specifics for his tax policy and his support of the Brady Bill to curb gun violence but centered the conversation on race relations. Clinton spoke about visiting the church that Hall attends, speaking with his pastor, visiting schools, and the lack of opportunity for Black youth. He kept the focus on inequity and race but offered a hopeful vision for America. Clinton added, "The only way you ever really rebuilt a country is to invest in its people." Clinton advocated education reforms that included widespread availability of higher education loans, strengthening vocational programs, funding for Head Start in public schools, and computers in classrooms. Of course, Clinton navigated the personal alongside the political. He addressed his infamous "I didn't inhale" gaffe (when asked by a reporter whether he had tried marijuana) and he and Hillary Clinton – who joined him for the second half of the interview – briefly weighed in the trivial things that couples commonly argue about. Hillary also stayed on message and steered the conversation away from their marriage and back to race relations. The Clintons maintained a message of investment, investment in people – particularly Black Americans. The interview with Hall, an entertainer with credibility in the Black community, conveyed candidate authenticity with nonwhite voters and enabled the Clinton campaign to build a coalition of Black supporters. The campaign strategy paid off at the polls, with Clinton receiving 83% of the Black vote in the 1992 U.S. presidential election (Roper, 2022). Incidentally, Clinton normalized the late-night television circuit for presidential campaigns and helped reimagine how the public perceives presidential behavior. He demonstrated that a candidate could not only be issues focused but also be playful, energetic, and relatable to the average American.

By the 2000 U.S. presidential campaign, candidates had plenty of time to ponder the successes of a two-term President Clinton, while grappling with an electorate even less attentive to news media as household adoption rates of the internet exceeded 50% for the first time (Pew, 2021). This year marked a pivotal election for political campaign communication, with soft news and late-night television in the limelight. The race featured presidential candidates appearing on *The Tonight Show With Jay Leno*, *Late Night With David Letterman*, *The Daily Show With Jon Stewart*, and MTV programs. And during the gaffe-prone Bush presidency from 2000 to 2008, the influence of Comedy Central's more satirical programming, *The Colbert Report* and *The Daily Show*, further expanded the audience for late-night television and offered a fresh format that especially resonated with young men.

The political campaign strategy for appearances in these comedic spaces builds on the daytime television importance of using political narratives to help personalize the campaign and establish relatability with politically inattentive audiences but requires an additional layer or, for some candidates, an additional obstacle. The candidate must demonstrate their ability to match wits and humor the host and audience. In other words, the candidate must adapt to the comedic space. It is a lesson Bush and Obama learned quickly.

Bush embraced the self-deprecating humor which conveyed a folksy, relatable, and fallible man to voters. In other words, the imperfection of Bush was part of the appeal. Critics of Bush often pointed to his lackluster academic performance in college; transcripts from Yale University revealed that the candidate was a "C" student. This criticism presented the ideal context for David Letterman's "Top 10 List" segment. On a *Tonight Show* appearance during the 2000 campaign, Bush read aloud the Top 10 List with the theme being the top changes he would make in the White House. At No. 7, Bush read, "Make sure the White House library has lots of books with big print and pictures." The punchline played well with the live studio audience, with both guest and host sharing a laugh that demonstrated Bush's ability shrug off criticism and that, despite his storied and privileged upbringing in Texas, he was still human.

In a 2005 visit on *The Daily Show*, Obama – then Senator from Illinois – joined a live feed from Washington to primarily tout his new book, *Dreams From My Father*. The appearance introduced Obama's charismatic and relaxed demeanor to a national audience. Obama made a few jabs at Congressional gridlock, and when the conversation moved from punchlines levied at Congress to punchlines levied toward him, he demonstrated that he could rub elbows with the comedic host. When Jon Stewart asked Obama to address the hype around the senator, Obama quipped, "The only person more over-hyped than me is you." The candid counter joke took Stewart, who could not contain his laughter, by surprise and resulted in a moment of mutual respect and audience cheers. Obama's ability to match wits conveyed to voters a fast-thinking and confident candidate – a candidate with the charisma to charm even the most cynical of comedians. Importantly, the visit on *The Daily Show* helped campaigns understand the importance of the indirect campaign, the necessity of introducing candidates to the national political stage long before filing election papers. Late-night television was now a vehicle for introducing rising stars within a political party.

In a similar trajectory, Donald Trump utilized entertainment media to indirectly campaign a few years before seeking the presidency. Already a household name for his wealth and *The Apprentice*, voters knew little about his political views or ambitions. In a 2013 appearance on *Late Night With David Letterman*, Trump – who *The New York Times* reported was then considering running for governor as a springboard for a presidential campaign – shirked off Letterman's question about whether he would seek office (Craig & Chen, 2016). Trump quickly shifted the conversation not to the challenges facing New York but to the challenges facing Washington. He spoke disparagingly about Congress and the polarization between the two parties. He criticized those working in Washington, calling the system a "mess." Trump used the interview to characterize himself as an outsider, an anti-establishment beltway repair man. The quick refocusing of the conversation from state politics to Washington politics reinforced his national political ambitions and the interview strategically re-introduced Trump to a national audience, but this time through the frame of a political leader rather than a reality television star. The Obama and Trump's examples demonstrate the critical role late-night television can play in shaping campaigns at the exploratory level, but soft news programs have also emerged as critical tools for more direct political campaign communication.

Democrat John Edwards was the first to directly launch a presidential campaign on late-night television, making the announcement on *The Daily Show* in 2003. Most voters in the 2008 U.S. presidential election knew Fred Thompson as Judge Arthur Branch, from NBC's *Law & Order*. Nonetheless, Thompson's diverse career quite effectively melded entertainment with politics. He worked as an attorney, represented Tennessee in the U.S. Senate, and would mount a run for the White House – with help from late-night television. In September 2007, Thompson officially announced his campaign on *The Tonight Show with Jay Leno*. For a traditional Southern Republican, the venue made sense strategically. Leno's audience skewed older and whiter, with a higher concentration of rural viewers than competing late-night programs (Zakarin, 2013). Importantly, the television studio was a place of comfort for the seasoned actor; the audience enthusiastically received the news of his candidacy and his appearance served as a precursor to a 15-minute campaign announcement released on his website. Although unsuccessful in securing the party's nomination, Thompson placed so much stock in the importance of entertainment media that he reportedly chose to forgo a primary debate hosted by the University of New Hampshire to tape with Leno (Allen, 2007).

Candidates can leverage entertaining soft news programs for a variety of strategic goals. Democratic candidate Bernie Sanders strategically timed appearances on *The View* and *The Late Show With Stephen Colbert* to build momentum from a strong New Hampshire primary victory in 2016, using the programs to tout his economic policies and appeal to moderate women and young men. In an August 2018 interview on *The Late Show With Stephen Colbert*, Democratic candidate Cory Booker foreshadowed to viewers that he would be "running for something" in 2020. Booker used the appearance as a chance to reinforce his values: his desire to restore unity and coalition building to Washington. And with the blending of the personal with political being hyper important in the entertainment space, Booker would be remiss if he neglected to talk about his *Dungeons & Dragons* hobby. During his first year in office, Obama become the second sitting president to directly speak with the American public through a soft news program. (Bush appeared in a sit-down interview with Dr. Phil in 2004 to mainly discuss parenting styles).

Late-night television serves a dual purpose: to advance political campaigns while humanizing the candidates. The late-night talk format provides a less scripted venue for candidates to frame their public personas and communicate relatability and authenticity to voters. Late-night television is the ideal blending of the political and the personal, a platform to reach inattentive voters but effective use of this venue also requires that politicians learn to comfortably exchange barbs with quick-witted hosts. Beyond advancing candidates, soft news can also serve as an instrument for policymaking.

The policymaking implications of soft news

Amidst challenging economic times in 2009, Obama became the first-sitting president to appear on late-night television. Following the subprime mortgage crisis and 2008 housing market crash, the president utilized *The Tonight Show With Jay Leno* to push for financial sector reforms. Obama was critical of Wall Street, referencing colossal bonuses and the culture of "entitlement." He defended the fiscal policies of his treasury secretary and promised reforms. By all accounts, the policy goals he laid out were well received by the audience. Nonetheless, news headlines weren't focused on policy but, rather, an offhanded joke that resulted in a rare gaffe for the first-term president. As Leno steered the conversation away from fiscal policy to sports, the topic of the president's subpar bowling score came up. In an attempt at self-deprecating humor, which typically scores well in the soft news format, Obama compared his bowling score to something akin to a Special Olympics score. Headlines in *NBC, ABC, The LA Times, Reuters,* and other news outlets focused on the offensive joke – and the president's apology – rather than the policy points. The novel maneuver of speaking directly with the American public through late-night television underscored the risks associated with the entertaining platform. The gaffe ultimately muted much of Obama's economic policy agenda. The informal structure of these late-night television appearances can be challenging venues for advancing policy as they are often unpredictable in talking points or tone. President Joe Biden faced similar challenges in 2022.

President Biden's visit on *Jimmy Kimmel Live* was an opportunity to address public concerns about escalating inflation and the U.S. Supreme Court's overturning of Roe. V. Wade. Kimmel, a self-professed Democrat who voted for Biden, engaged the president's policy conversation, including a timely discussion on gun violence in the aftermath of the Uvalde, Texas school shooting that left 21 dead. A visibly frustrated Kimmel pressed Biden on the inaction of Washington in addressing gun violence. Biden seemed aloof relative to the host's fire on the issue. Kimmel questioned Biden's fight, leadership, and overly optimistic candor on gun reforms. The interview's tone suggested that the comedian was more impassioned over gun violence than the president. And when defending his optimism about the future, Biden referenced an increase in biracial couples depicted on television commercials as a reason to be hopeful, echoing a statement he made one year earlier at a June 1, 2021, speech in remembrance of the Tulsa race massacre. The comments were tone deaf and fodder for internet memes that were further amplified across right-wing media and digital platforms including the Republican National Committee's *War Room* YouTube channel.

Much like the blockbuster model of filmmaking is often high risk/high reward for studios, the same could be said of using soft news to advance policy goals, particularly across late-night television, where hosts are less predictable and preoccupied with landing laughs. But Obama was more adept at leveraging soft news for advancing policy by his second term, and his appearances on talk-format programs would be more effective when educating the public on the Affordable Care Act.

Between Two Ferns, a comedic talk program hosted by Zach Galifianakis, welcomed Obama on March 13, 2014. The show, featured on digital comedy network Funny or Die, attracted an especially young audience and essentially parodied the talk-format genre of network television. From the onset, Obama molded his communication style to match the deadpan humor of Galifianakis. Barbs were exchanged over the president's birth certificate and the host's *Hangover* series – which Obama claimed Bradley Cooper carried – without either of them cracking a smile. When Galifianakis asked Obama how it feels when others let him win at basketball, the president fired back with: "How does it feel having a 3-inch vertical?" The comedian corrected the president, noting, "It's a 3-inch horizontal." The adversarial word play had the audience entertained and served as a segue for plugging healthcare.gov, the website used to enroll people in health insurance provided through the Affordable Care Act. He addressed problems with the enrollment rollout but provided viewers multiple ways to sign up. The interview was reportedly brokered between Bradley Cooper and White House Senior Advisor Valerie Jarrett after the two met at a state dinner (Dovere & Budoff Brown, 2014). With a reach of more than 44 million views on YouTube, the healthcare.gov website benefited from a 40% increase in traffic after the guest appearance, helping the administration reach its sign up targets (Judah, 2014; Dovere & Budoff Brown, 2014).

U.S. Senator Chris Murphy (D-Connecticut) and former Texas congressman Beto O'Rourke also struck the right chord when leveraging soft news to advance gun reforms in the days following the Uvalde, Texas shooting in 2022. Murphy went beyond the traditional news circuit to communicate his policy goals to the public and maintain persistent pressure on other political elites to act on gun legislation. Murphy included a pit stop on *Late Night With Seth Myers* to push for bipartisan congressional support for gun reform. Murphy pressed on, with an appearance on *The Late Show With Stephen Colbert*. Murphy drew comparisons between the Sandy Hook and Uvalde shootings. He politely indulged in the host's sidestepping to more light-hearted banter, professing his love for the Klondike choco tacos, but kept the conversation fixated on the policy problem. O'Rourke paralleled Murphy's strategic use of soft news, making appearances on late-night television and daytime talk programs, putting relentless pressure on other political elites, notably Texas Governor Greg Abbott. Murphy and O'Rourke tapped another useful strategy for soft news: political narratives. They often spoke on the gun issue not through the lens of a legislator but from the more personal lens of a parent with young children. They weren't speaking on behalf of a political party but were instead speaking on behalf of children, on behalf of parents. On June 23, 2022, President Biden signed into law the first major federal gun legislation in nearly 30 years, expanding background checks and incentivizing states to adopt more stringent gun laws.

Teenage activists from Parkland, Florida, leveraged a similar soft news strategy when advancing stricter gun legislation policy following the school shooting at Stoneham Douglas High School. The activists, led by Emma Gonzalez and David Hogg, made numerous appearances on daytime talk shows and late-night television to keep gun violence among the top priorities for the public and legislators. Their activism was credited for playing a critical role in increasing the age to buy firearms in Florida and the state legislature banning the sales of bump stocks, attachments that replace standard stocks and allow for more rapid fire of semiautomatic weapons. Whether it's influence on a smaller scale in a state legislature, or advancing reforms on the federal level, the issue of gun violence underscores the role that entertainment media can play in keeping a policy issue in the news cycle and maintaining public pressure on political elites.

You may wonder how one could argue that daytime talk and late-night television programs remain a campaign imperative or even a policymaking tool when younger generations are more likely to stream content than tune in to traditional broadcast networks. Just how effective can strategic use of those programs be for political campaigns when audiences are incredibly fragmented?

Assessing the campaign effectiveness of soft news

Although news outlets have yielded a great deal of its influence to entertainment media, scholars have found some civically desirable outcomes of campaigning through soft news. For example, incidental exposure to political issues on entertaining programs can improve viewer knowledge and increase motivation to follow those issues in the news (Hardy et al., 2014; Becker & Bode, 2018). Despite viewers' primary motivations for consuming soft news being centered on entertainment, some also report feeling more informed after exposure to these programs, and that may result in higher levels of **political efficacy**, or the extent to which people feel empowered to engage, understand, and influence their government (Roth et al., 2014). Others have found that consuming infotainment elevates levels of political engagement and increases viewer intent to vote (Moy et al., 2005; Baum & Jamison, 2006).

A common thread of research examining civic effects of entertainment media is that it is most beneficial to **low information voters**, meaning those less attentive to politics and political campaigns. These low information voters are also more likely to be moderate or apolitical in their thinking, less tethered to a political party or ideology. Consequently, these low information voters are often more persuadable than partisan voters. Even if exposure does not ultimately translate to votes, these appearances seem to, at the very least, humanize candidates. Research has shown that strategic use of late-night television can prime audiences to consider the character traits of candidates (Moy et al., 2006). In other words, soft news creates strategic opportunities for campaigns to craft political narratives for their candidate's public persona, introducing them to potential voters that would otherwise be ill-motivated to seek information about them.

The timing of these appearances is also critical. Candidates may appear early in the campaign process or long before officially launching a campaign, to begin building name recognition and testing public reaction. These appearances are not only useful in brokering introductions between a candidate and the electorate but also necessary in maintaining momentum. Several candidates have strategically timed appearances to coincide with a surge in polls or a strong showing in a state primary race. For example, Bernie Sanders scheduled appearances on *The View* and *Late Show With Stephen Colbert* just days following his 2016 primary victory in New Hampshire, seizing the opportunity to tout his economic views and appeal to less attentive voters. In other words, momentum building is another strategic use of soft news programs.

To engage with less political audiences most effectively, Parkin (2014) notes the importance of blending the personal with the political; his research shows that this balance of content resonates best with audiences for candidates of either political party. Candidate appearances on daytime talk shows are evenly split between personal conversation and policy talk, whereas late-night television appearances lean 55% policy driven and 45% personal (Parkin, 2014). This means that soft news programs are ripe for personalized political narratives and issue advocacy. But, first and foremost, audiences are tuned in to be entertained.

Another incentive for candidate appearances is the inherent tone of the soft news programs. Hosts approach these interviews from a more neutral posture. The soft news environment is more welcoming and less aggressive, although that doesn't mean that the interviews aren't substantive or avoid tough questions. Nonetheless, candidates appearing on entertainment programs are typically treated with more neutrality (Lichter et al., 2014; Parkin, 2014). Campaigns may perceive less risk in candidate appearances on soft news programs that are less negatively toned than interviews with mainstream news outlets. And research finds that humor on late-night television is event (or gaffe) driven and not especially partisan or biased (Lichter et al., 2014).

Even as the mass audience for network television has diminished in recent decades, amplification effects across news media and social media underscore the continued importance of engaging with infotainment. Moments on soft news programs often appear in the mainstream news cycle and circulate across social networking platforms. For example, when late-night television host Jimmy Fallon touched Donald Trump's hair to prove its authenticity during the 2016 campaign, it quickly surfaced in the mainstream news cycle and generated national news headlines for *The Atlantic*, *The Chicago Tribune*, *The Detroit News*, *Time*, *Vanity Fair*, and *Slate*, while circulating social media and appearing in several local affiliate news broadcasts. Soft news moments maintain longevity as appearances are amplified through shares, likes, and comments across social media.

Summary

The evolutionary shift from campaigning within the limits of traditional news media to embracing entertaining media was a slow burn. Despite Kennedy and Nixon making late-night television appearances during the 1960 presidential campaign, entertainment media was not widely embraced as campaign strategy and candidates were reluctant to adapt to the entertaining culture of the mediums. Shifts in the U.S. media landscape made this political communication pathway to entertainment media possible, but the success of Clinton's 1992 campaign and Bush's 2000 campaign played an especially influential role in demonstrating the potential of campaigning through soft news. Those campaigns provided a blueprint for future candidates navigating the entertainment space and reduced the risks associated with adapting to those platforms.

From 1992 to 2004, the number of presidential candidate appearances on soft news shows tripled to 27, and by the 2008 U.S. presidential campaign, that number reached 101 (Parkin, 2014). Today, campaigns have chosen entertainment over news media, bypassing mainstream news outlets to reach the fragmented electorate. These critical appearances are not just about politics and policy. These forums give equal footing to the personal and help to establish perceived relatability of candidates – an increasingly important consideration for low-information voters in today's ubiquitous media environment.

Resources and references

Allen, M. (2007, September 5). Fred Thompson finally announces run. *Politico*. www.politico.com/story/2007/09/fred-thompson-finally-announces-run-005665

Andrews, T. M. (2016, September 22). From Kennedy to Trump: The much-deplored history of presidential candidates on late-night TV. *The Washington Post*. www.washingtonpost.com/news/morning-mix/wp/2016/09/22/from-jfk-to-nixon-to-trump-presidential-candidates-and-their-goofiness-on-late-night-tv/

Baum, M. A. (2005). Talking the vote: Why presidential candidates hit the talk show circuit. *American Journal of Political Science*, *49*(2), 213–234.

Baum, M. A., & Jamison, A. S. (2006). The Oprah effect: How soft news helps inattentive citizens vote consistently. *Journal of Politics*, *68*(4), 946–959.

Becker, A. B., & Bode, L. (2018). Satire as a source for learning? The differential impact of news versus satire exposure on net neutrality knowledge gain. *Information, Communication & Society*, *21*(4), 612–625.

Craig, S., & Chen, D. (2016, March 5). Donald Trump considered path to presidency starting at governor's mansion in New York. *The New York Times*. www.nytimes. com/2016/03/06/nyregion/donald-trump-new-york-governor.html

Dovere, E., & Budoff Brown, C. (2014, April 2). Behind the Obamacare surprise. *Politico*. www.politico.com/story/2014/04/obamacare-affordable-care-act-enrollment-105275

FitzSimons, A. (2019, May 22). How "The View" became the most important political TV show in America. *The New York Times Magazine*. www.nytimes.com/2019/05/22/ magazine/the-view-politics-tv.html

Hardy, B. W., Gottfried, J. A., Winneg, K. M., & Hall Jamieson, K. (2014). Stephen Colbert's civics lesson: How Colbert Super PAC taught viewers about campaign finance. *Mass Communication & Society*, *17*(3), 329–353.

Judah, S. (2014, March 12). #BBCtrending: Did between two ferns really help Obamacare? *BBC*. www.bbc.com/news/blogs-trending-26547571

Kimmel, J. [Jimmy Kimmel Live]. (2022, June 8). *President Joe Biden visits Jimmy Kimmel live* [Video]. YouTube. www.youtube.com/watch?v=ZEtPV-qvLe8

Lichter, S. R., Baumgartner, J. C., & Morris, J. S. (2014). *Politics is a joke! How TV comedians are remaking political life*. Routledge.

Moy, P., Xenos, M. A., & Hess, V. K. (2005). Communication and citizenship: Mapping the political effects of infotainment. *Mass Communication & Society*, *8*(2), 111–131.

Moy, P., Xenos, M. A., & Hess, V. K. (2006). Priming effects of late-night comedy. *International Journal of Public Opinion Research*, *18*(2), 198–210.

MrAssassinscreed47. (2020, December 13). *Oprah Winfrey show, September 19, 2000* [Video]. YouTube. www.youtube.com/watch?v=oKRN9s5OPKE

Obama, B. [Funny or Die]. (2014, March 13). *President Barack Obama: Between two ferns with Zach Galifianakis* [Video]. YouTube. www.youtube.com/ watch?v=UnW3xkHxIEQ

Parkin, M. (2014). *Talk show campaigns: Presidential candidates on daytime and late night television*. Routledge.

Pew. (2021, April 7). *Internet broadband fact sheet*. Pew Research Center. www.pewresearch.org/internet/fact-sheet/internet-broadband/

Roper Center for Public Opinion Research. (2022). *How groups voted in 1992: US elections*. https://ropercenter.cornell.edu/how-groups-voted-1992

Roth, F. S., Weinmann, C., Schneider, F. M., Hopp, F. R., & Vorderer, P. (2014). Seriously entertained: Antecedents and consequences of hedonic and eudaimonic entertainment experiences with political talk shows on TV. *Mass Communication & Society*, *17*(3), 354–378.

Wagmeister, E. (2022, August 16). The view tops daytime talk show ratings for 2021–2022 season. *Variety*. https://variety.com/2022/tv/news/the-view-ratings-2021-2022-1235342918/

Zakarin, J. (2013, May 29). Jay Leno viewers are old, male and live in middle America. *Buzzfeed News*. www.buzzfeed.com/jordanzakarin/jay-leno-viewers-are-old-male-and-live-in-middle-america

4 Sitcoms and satire
The art of the political cameo

The first televised presidential debates featured John F. Kennedy and Richard Nixon during the 1960 election. Kennedy embraced the new medium, wore make up, looked intently at the camera when speaking, and appeared relaxed during the debate. Nixon, on the other hand, refused make-up, looked pale under the studio lighting, and perspired. Those watching the debate believed Kennedy outperformed Nixon, whereas those listening on the radio felt Nixon performed better. This divergence in public opinion was attributed to a concept known as **medium theory**, when the platform or technology a message is delivered through shapes audience interpretation of the content. In other words, the visual emphasis of the television altered public perception of the two candidates' debate performance. The problem for Nixon was that television was now the medium of the present and future. Nixon wouldn't make the same mistake twice.

When seeking the presidency again eight years later, Nixon reluctantly turned to entertainment television. The guarded former vice president and senator of California took a two-year hiatus from granting interviews to prominent news programs *Meet the Press* and *Face the Nation* and his campaign was tasked with mitigating a public image of the candidate as dry, serious, and humorless (Daugherty, 2018). Despite some objections from staffers due to the show's counterculture themes, Nixon appeared in a 5-second cameo on *Rowan & Martin's Laugh-In* – the top comedy program in 1968. Nixon awkwardly delivered the show's catchphrase, "Sock it to me!" on camera. Due to federal **equal time laws**, which requires broadcasters to offer equivalent airtime to opposition candidates, NBC also extended an invitation to Democrat Hubert Humphrey to appear on the program. Humphrey declined and some political analysts believed that Nixon's cameo effectively softened his dull public image and helped elect him to the White House (Daugherty, 2018; Foggatt, 2019).

As campaigns uneasily grappled with television over the next few decades, most candidates avoided entertainment programs. Cameos in satirical shows, situational comedies, and television dramas were not only rare, but they were also unheard of. Even by the 1990s the notion of a national political figure making a cameo on scripted television shows was so incredibly rare that CBS hyped up Republican Georgia Senator New Gingrich's guest appearance on *Murphy*

DOI: 10.4324/9781003364832-4

Brown almost a year in advance, airing teasers promising a "rumble" between Gingrich and the titular character of the show, a tough news anchor. The hype underscored the novelty of this intersection between entertainment and politics but Gingrich's guest appearance, which included a few brief lines, also signaled the beginning of a new campaign era that broke down the more rigid decorum of candidates and invited the **political cameo**, when a candidate or prominent politician appears in a fictional show or film playing themselves.

As fleeting as a political cameo is, they serve a strategic purpose in humanizing the candidate and spotlighting policy issues. As audiences fragmented and became less attentive to news, satirical programs such as *The Daily Show* and *The Colbert Report* exploded in popularity. These satirical news programs expedited the acceptance of the intersection between politics and entertainment, essentially reducing the political risks of candidate appearances in comedic formats. From John McCain to Joe Biden, the rise in appearances on television sitcoms and dramas suggests that political cameos now serve as strategic mainstays that improve a politician's relatability and allow them to reach less engaged voters. And no single program has accommodated more political cameos than the comedy sketch show *Saturday Night Live*.

SNL and the live political cameo

With HBO's dark comedy *The White Lotus*, a surprise hit of 2022, it wasn't surprising that *Saturday Night Live* tapped actress Aubrey Plaza to host the first episode of 2023. Plaza, known for her deadpan role on the sitcom *Parks and Recreation*, is a native of the small state of Delaware – as is President Joe Biden. During Plaza's opening monologue, she indirectly references a 2018 poll proclaiming her to be the most famous person from Delaware; Biden ranked sixth. Plaza then cued up a video cameo from Biden. "Aubrey, you're the most famous person out of Delaware and there's no question about that. We're just grateful you made it out of White Lotus alive," Biden quipped, alluding to the show's twisted plots. The president, who would be seeking reelection in 2024, followed the political cameo with a tweet referencing his *SNL* appearance and included a clip of the monologue and caption reading: "Just two Delawareans, live from New York."

Although Biden was the most recent sitting president to appear on the comedy sketch show, Gerald Ford was the first, and the NBC show – a pop culture institution – has since played a prominent role in the road to political office, particularly in the last few election cycles.

The first season of *SNL* premiered in 1975, featuring a quirky cast of comedians and sketch writers creating live bits that parodied politicians, offered social commentary and introduced zany characters all held together by a rotating host and musical guest. The show has welcomed more than 20 presidents and presidential candidates. Ford, who abruptly took office following Nixon's resignation, remained relatively unknown to the American public. In seeking reelection in 1976, his campaign had little to lose by engaging with entertainment media, particularly given that he was unelected and the relationship between the news media and the White House was significantly strained following the Watergate scandal (Cramer Brownell, 2016). Ford made a brief cameo to deliver the signature "Live from New York" line before the show's opening credits. The opportunity arose after Ford's press secretary Ron Nessen invited comedian Chevy Chase, who impersonated Ford on *SNL*, to a White House dinner with the president. *SNL* tapped Nessen to host and Ford came along for the cameo.

Despite the novel campaign appearance, the media were critical of Nessen hosting the program, and the cameo was not enough to defeat Democrat Jimmy Carter. Nonetheless, the maneuver turned entertaining spaces into "political battlefields" (Cramer Brownell, 2016). Much has evolved for the art of the political cameo since Nixon and Ford's appearances. First, the frequency of political cameos has increased in the era of media abundance. Second, cameos today are much longer, with politicians taking on scripted lines and integrating into the plot and sketches or tapped for hosting responsibilities. In the context of *SNL*, aired live, the program also tests a candidate's performative abilities under pressure.

Numerous politicians from across the ideological spectrum have made appearances on the show, with the frequency of political cameos ramping up in the 2004 U.S. presidential election. In addition to Ford and Biden, *SNL* has welcomed Hillary Clinton, Donald Trump, Chris Christie, Jon Huntsman, Barack Obama, Al Sharpton, Al Gore, Bob Dole, John McCain, Steve Forbes, Rudy Giuliani, George Pataki, George H. W. Bush, Jesse Jackson, George McGovern, Ralph Nader, Sarah Palin, Elizabeth Warren, and Bernie Sanders. Most of the cameos were more involved than the single-line delivery that Ford appeared for. Candidate cameos in recent election cycles have come with the caveat and pressure of letting lose and participating in sketches. In today's landscape of media abundance, flashing a face or delivering a single tag line isn't enough to generate news coverage and online buzz, but those who deliver punchlines under pressure of live television will earn some notice. The expectations of these cameos evolved after Republican John McCain became the first-sitting senator to host the show in 2002 (**see Case Study 4.1**). With McCain, a future presidential candidate going all in as host, the pressure would be on other politicians to be more involved in entertainment media.

Appearances on the program's satirical news segment, "Weekend Update," are one way that politicians reach the politically inattentive. The format allows for banter with the hosts and an opportunity to generate viral moments. A few years before his 2016 presidential campaign, New Jersey Governor Chris Christie executed a cameo in the aftermath of Hurricane Sandy. The Republican appeared confident and delivered sarcastic nods to the people of his home state, including jokes about New Jersey people being known for their patience. The segment included self-deprecating humor about the fleece jacket

Case Study 4.1   McCain becomes first-sitting U.S. Senator to Host *SNL*

Figure 4.1   John McCain plays himself in an *SNL* sketch opposite Tina Fey, one of his several cameos on the show as both U.S. Senator and presidential candidate.

Source: Illustration by Eduardo Rangel.

Arizona Senator John McCain, who launched presidential campaigns in 2000 and 2008, became the first-sitting U.S. Senator to host *SNL* in 2002. National-level politicians had made brief appearances in the past, but hosting would take the political cameo to a new level, requiring delivery of a monologue, introduction of the musical performer, and acting in scripted sketches. McCain appeared comfortable on camera during his monologue, which received a comedic boost from Fred Armisen playing a quirky Venezuelan comedian. McCain appeared in several sketches. He played a clingy, cringy spouse in a Lifetime movie parody; himself in a *Meet the Press* parody; and adopted an Irish accent for a pub sketch. McCain could be self-deprecating in one scene, and goofy in the next. McCain's hosting drew supportive reviews, and he displayed a humble gravitas of sorts. Being a pioneer in his embrace of entertainment media also suited the maverick persona that his campaigns so often cultivated. McCain would later resurface in additional cameos on *SNL*. Appearing as a presidential candidate in 2008, his *SNL* cold opens encouraged people to vote. He also played himself in a QVC sketch opposite Tina Fey (as Sarah Palin, of course), selling campaign merch including a chatty Joe Biden action figure. The cameos shifted campaign norms and allowed the senator to carve a name for himself among a national audience. McCain's ability to "be a good sport" and put aside partisanship for comedic relief attracted supporters from all political spectrums, making him beloved by members of both parties. Once a relatively unknown politician McCain's name recognition and favorability improved following his *SNL* hosting debut and his continued engagement with entertainment. By the time of his second campaign for president, he was recognized by 90% of Americans and McCain had a 58% favorability rating one year prior to his death (Dugan, 2018). McCain's cameos also helped to shape his legacy after his death. On September 1, 2018, *SNL* re-aired that 2002 episode he hosted and numerous news outlets across the country referenced his SNL cameos in their coverage commemorating his life and service.

he seemingly always wore in media footage of the governor's clean-up efforts. Christie exuded state pride, jostled wits with comedian Seth Myers and quoted a song by Bruce Springsteen – the "boss" of New Jersey. Christie charmed the audience, demonstrating that he had an entertaining side and could handle the performative pressure of live television. *SNL* cameos of the last 20 years have also called for politicians to participate in sketches and deliver punchlines.

While only appearing in a brief *SNL* cameo in 2008, Hillary Clinton did not pass on an opportunity for a more involved cameo in 2015 as she ramped up her second campaign for president. The sketch starts with a frustrated Clinton (impersonated by Kate McKinnon) slouched over a bar voicing her frustrations with the campaign and her impatience with becoming president. She asks the bartender to pour her another, when the real Clinton spins around and serves McKinnon another drink. McKinnon introduces herself as Clinton to bartender "Val" (the real Clinton). The back and forth between Clinton and her doppelgänger addressed many public criticisms including her sincerity, ambition, and voting record as a U.S. Senator, noting delayed positions on the keystone pipeline and delayed support for same-sex marriage. (McKinnon was the first openly lesbian cast member on *SNL*). The nearly 6-minute sketch, long by the program's standards, also afforded Clinton time to score Donald Trump zingers and impersonate her future general election opponent. The cameo showed that she could field criticism, defend her record, perform well on live television, and even carry a tune. Not to be out done in 2016, Trump hosted *SNL*.

In 2015, Trump hosted the program for the second time. With hosting come the responsibilities of delivering a monologue, appearing in a few sketches, introducing the musical guest, and occasionally appearing in pre-recorded digital shorts. Rather than building a monologue around self-deprecating humor that plays well for most candidates, the script (and teasers leading up to the episode) focused on self-aggrandizement and Trump's overconfidence. Trump's monologue drew few laughs from the studio audience and critics and, even some cast members, ranked it among *SNL*'s worst episodes (St. James & Framke, 2015). The selection of Trump to host also sparked online criticism and threats of boycotting the show. Trump was utilized in some sketches, often delivering brief lines near the end of a scene but one key highlight came from a pre-recorded digital short parodying Drake's "Hotline Bling" music video. The video generated significant online buzz.

Strategically timed just a few days ahead of a pivotal New Hampshire primary election, Democratic candidate and Vermont Senator Bernie Sanders made a cameo in a February 2016 episode. Appearing in the "Steam Ship" sketch alongside comedian Larry David, who regularly impersonates Sanders, the politician interjects as David's character protests the women and children first policy for evacuating the passengers from the sinking ship to the lifeboats. David plays up his wealth to jump the line and here is when Sanders begins deriding the "1%" and their "preferential treatment." This was a common theme of the Sanders campaign. The line not only served as a reminder of Sanders' values but also made light of his often-repeated campaign talking points. Sanders and David also debated the particulars of socialism and the pronunciation of the word "huge" (as Sanders rarely pronounces the letter h). The senator won the New Hampshire primary in a landslide a few days following the episode.

Given that the show is broadcasted at Rockefeller Center in New York, *SNL* has also provided a platform for New York mayors looking to advance to higher office. Gregarious mayor Ed Koch made four political cameos on the program, including two times as host. His first appearance came in 1978, just a few years before his unsuccessful campaign to become the state's governor in 1982. David Dinkins made a brief cameo on the program in 1993, contributing to an *Aladdin* sketch. David Paterson delivered cameos both as mayor of New York and twice as governor of the state. Paterson, blind and the first Black governor of New York, drew attention to problematic portrayals of blind people on the program, delivered bold punchlines, and shaped the narrative of his tenure by highlighting policy achievements including a balanced budget. With eyes on a future presidential campaign, Michael Bloomberg also appeared on the program in his final term as mayor. Mayor and future presidential candidate Rudy Giuliani was especially involved in the program. He hosted as mayor in 1997, performing in drag, and anchoring multiple sketches. His appearance was well received by critics, who noted that Giuliani executed comedic moments well and the hosting duties help humanize the politician. Importantly, Giuliani was front and center for *SNL*'s return after 9/11.

The mayor made a somber cameo during the monologue of the show that aired on September 29, 2001. Appearing alongside *SNL* creator and producer Lorne Michaels, with members of the New York fire and police departments in the backdrop, Giuliani paid tribute to first responders, the people of New York and its institutions. Musician Paul Simon played a moving rendition of "The Boxer" – an unofficial ode to the city. Giuliani stressed the importance of reopening New York institutions, adding, "*Saturday Night Live* is one of our great New York City institutions, and that's why it's important for you do your show tonight." Michaels asked, "Can we be funny?" and Giuliani rhetorically quipped, "Why start now?" The two embraced with a gentle hug as Giuliani delivered the "Live from New York, it's Saturday night" line. Giuliani was seen as a calming force and leader in a moment of crisis during the aftermath of 9/11. He appeared "presidential" and this moment on the national stage helped make Giuliani a household name and early frontrunner to be the Republican nominee in the 2008 presidential election.

SNL cameos demonstrate that comedy can help campaigns reach large audiences while humanizing candidates; however, it's not always easily executed for a group of people who are not natural entertainers. Self-deprecating humor and ease on screen are essential to making a cameo appear authentic and unforced. Taped sitcoms provide a platform for political candidates to do just that but without the pressure of live television.

Prime-time juggernauts: sitcoms and cameos

Shortly after Bill Clinton moved the needle on acceptable decorum for presidential candidates, with his *Arsenio Hall Show* appearance in 1992, political campaign communication expanded significantly to the realm of entertainment media. In the 1990s, prominent politicians began to dabble with scripted television programs, arranging political cameos on popular network sitcoms. The 30-minute format typically calls for taping in front of a live studio audience, sometimes with prompted laugh tracks. Plots are simplistic, with predictable tropes and universal themes that appeal to broad audiences. The sitcom cameo has been tapped as another campaign tool used by politicians looking to build name recognition and, at times, by those actively campaigning.

One of the earliest examples is U.S. Senator from Massachusetts John Kerry in the NBC's *Cheers*, a sitcom set in a Boston pub. In an episode that aired in 1992, characters "Norm" and "Cliff" are walking in Boston when they recognize Kerry on the street. They stare for a while and then approach him to request an autograph. When they make a comment about Kerry being good enough for the national news desk, Kerry realizes it is a case of mistaken identity and explains that he is a U.S. Senator – not a local news reporter. Disappointed, the two characters apologize, nix their request for the autograph, and continue down the street. The self-deprecating plot of a prominent politician going unrecognized by characters has since become a common trope of the political cameo, often showcasing humility that humanizes the politician. The cameo helped introduce Kerry to a national audience relatively early in his political career; he would later run for president in 2004 and serve as secretary of state under the Obama administration. At the time of his cameo, *Cheers* was reaching an audience of close to 30 million people.

Mayor Giuliani (and future presidential hopeful) tapped into another wildly popular sitcom to elevate his national exposure. Giuliani's appearance on *Seinfeld* included brief scripted lines, and the scene was well integrated into the plot. The 1993 cameo appeared in an episode in which the *Seinfeld* characters realized that non-fat yogurt was not in fact fat-free. The revelation created an uproar in the city, prompting Giuliani's public address: "I promise you, my fellow New Yorkers, that Mayor Giuliani will do everything possible to cleanse the city of this falsified non-fat yogurt." That non-fat yogurt episode drew in more than 31 million viewers, and Giuliani would remain a fixture in the national political arena for decades to come, even coming close to securing the Republican Party's nomination in the 2008 presidential election.

Despite their role in brokering large-scale introductions between a politician and a national audience, cameos remained an underused method of connecting with the electorate throughout the 1990s. Although Clinton helped remove some of the political risk associated with appearances on entertainment television, it took time for candidates to be comfortable doing so. The political cameo remained so novel in 1996 that CBS teased Republican Newt Gingrich's appearance on *Murphy Brown* for nearly a year (Waxman, 1996). At the time of the cameo, Gingrich started serving as speaker of the house (and would launch a presidential campaign in 2012). In the episode, fictional news anchor Murphy Brown delivers a speech at a "Presscapade" political dinner. The speech included harsh punchlines directed at the politician and when Brown bumped into Gingrich at the event, she asked what he thought of the speech. Gingrich replies, "Oh, I can take a little ribbing," showing he can take a joke in stride. The political cameo was tame given the CBS trailers that promised a showdown of rhetorical punches between the fictional news anchor and Gingrich and given that former Vice President Dan Quayle publicly derided the show's lack of family values when the program plot had Brown pregnant and unwed. Nonetheless, conflict and controversy would defeat the purpose of the sitcom cameo, which is to demonstrate a lighter side of the politician and render them relatable to broad swaths of voters.

As a rule, the scripts accompanying political cameos seldom get heavy or confrontational. Mostly, they are introduced as a lesson in humility or as an opportunity for fictional characters to fangirl over a political figure.

For example, Hillary Clinton's March 2016 political cameo on Comedy Central's *Broad City* centered on a scene in which two characters working on Clinton's campaign unexpectedly have the chance to meet her. As the two characters reminisce about their campaign experience and walk through a Clinton campaign office, Clinton walks in the room. The encounter is met with awkward laughter and overexaggerated jaw-dropping expressions. As the characters fumble for the right words to say, Clinton just smiles and says, "It's alright, just take your time." Former Vice President Joe Biden – who ran for president in 1988, 2008, and 2020 – made more than one cameo on NBC's *Parks and Recreation*. In a 2012 episode, Leslie Knope's (the main character and head of a small-town parks department) fiancé surprises her with an engagement present: a meet and greet with Biden. Knope, who has a passion for public service and a not-so-secret crush on the VP, fawns over Biden. The cameo fits nicely into an already existing story arc, as Knope's fangirling on Biden was a reoccurring subtheme on the program. By melding the cameo into storylines, Biden appeared especially at ease and authentic, rather than forced.

Parks and Recreation has a lengthy track record of propping up people in public service. Presidential candidates and U.S. Senators Kirsten Gillibrand and Cory Booker appeared on the program, as did U.S. Senators Barbara Boxer and Olympia Snowe. John McCain appeared in two political cameos – the first featured him retrieving a jacket from a coatroom as Knope hides and cries in a closet because she is overwhelmed by her complicated Washington life. Here the punchline is that she doesn't recognize McCain's voice as her back is turned to him, and she orders him to leave the coatroom. Ahead of his presidential campaign, New Jersey Governor Chris Christie appeared on *The Michael J. Fox Show*, another NBC sitcom. Also preceding her run for the White House, U.S. Senator Elizabeth Warren made a cameo on the Amazon's *Alpha House*, a comedy focused on three Republican senators who room together in D.C. The 2014 cameo includes banter with John Goodman and helped introduce Warren to a national audience and plug her book, *A Fighting Chance*.

Although political cameos first surfaced across satirical programs and sitcoms, some politicians have also embraced television dramas, films, and reality television to bolster their national profiles.

Dramas, drag, and film: cameos that go beyond comedy

Television sitcoms provide an ideal platform for humanizing political candidates, but even across entertainment media, audiences are fragmented and tuned in to a wide variety of programming. Some campaigns take political cameos further by tapping into dramas. And doing so may also afford the candidate a more suitable platform for communicating serious policy positions.

BET drama *Being Mary Jane*, which first aired in 2014, centered around Black news anchor Paula Patterson (Gabrielle Union), as she navigated work–life balance in her journalism career. In Season 4 of the show, ahead of his 2020 campaign for president, U.S. Senator Cory Booker was included as a cameo in a scene that allowed him to deliver a policy point about the high rate of incarceration among Black Americans. In advance of his 2020 campaign, Vice President Biden made a cameo on NBC's *Law & Order: SVU* to raise awareness of the backlog of untested rape kits across police departments. Biden also tweeted about the cameo, directing viewers to ItsOnUs.org to learn more about a new White House sexual assault prevention program. Other cameos in more serious dramas can simply stem from relatable moments of fandom.

McCain wasn't shy about expressing his fandom for the action-drama *24* and fashioned himself to protagonist Jack Bauer (Kiefer Sutherland), an independent "maverick" type that aligned neatly with McCain's campaign narratives (Patterson, 2006). McCain proclaimed his endorsement of the show on Twitter, and he wasn't alone in his fandom; the suspenseful drama aired for nine seasons on Fox. With this popularity, it wasn't surprising that McCain's 2006 cameo – airing a year before launching his presidential campaign – on the show generated buzz. The cameo cut to a scene that showed McCain working at the fictional Counter Terrorist Unit delivering files to the character played by Kim Raver. An unusual 2010 cameo on the Discovery's *MythBusters* made the news cycle for President Obama, a self-described fan of the educational reality television show that deploys science and technology to debunk global myths. Obama reportedly watched the program with his daughters. In his cameo, the president asks the hosts to re-test the myth of Archimedes' solar death ray, a myth that suggests that the Greek mathematician set fire to Roman ships using mirrors and the heat of the sun. The cameo aired shortly before the launch of his reelection campaign.

These public displays of fandom help humanize politicians and make them appear authentic, grounded, and relatable. Of course, a candidate need not be a fan of the show to capitalize on the exposure that results from a well-timed cameo on a hit series.

Massachusetts Governor Michael Dukakis made a cameo on the NBC medical drama *St. Elsewhere* in 1985, a few years ahead of his 1988 presidential campaign. Dukakis appeared at the show's fictional hospital for treatment after twisting an ankle. Ahead of his 2016 campaign, former New York mayor Michael Bloomberg appeared for a political cameo in the season 4 finale of *The Good Wife*, a CBS drama about the life of a woman married to a corrupt politician caught up in sex scandal. The cameo called for Bloomberg to congratulate the fictional Illinois governor on winning the election. And although it was unclear at the time whether Hillary Clinton would run for president again in 2020, the former secretary of state made a cameo on season 5 of the CBS political drama *Madam Secretary*; she appeared opposite the fictional secretary of state Tea Leoni in the 2018 scene.

But over the last couple of decades, it's not scripted dramas that dominate prime-time television but reality television. Hosting *The Apprentice* was a big part of President Trump's campaign success by helping establish political narratives about his business acumen. The show, which aired for 14 seasons, called for contestants to complete business tasks to vie for a position in the Trump Organization. Consequently, Trump became a household name and pop culture icon. Many of his barbs and insults became part of the national vernacular. Trump even attempted to trademark "You're Fired!" He was one of the most recognizable faces on television and that name recognition would help him attract an avalanche of news attention when he announced his presidential campaign in 2015. The reality television cameo can be just as effective as appearances on scripted programs at generating water cooler talk on social media and infiltrating the news cycle.

Stakes were likely low at the time of California Congresswoman Nancy Pelosi's first cameo as a guest judge on *RuPaul's Drag Race* in 2018, a VH1 reality show in which drag queens compete in weekly contests organized by the iconic RuPaul. But the minority leader made a second surprise appearance on the show in 2022, demonstrating what some call her sarcastic "shade clap" (first delivered at a 2019 President Trump State of the Union address) and urging people to vote in the midterm elections – a midterm in which many analysts thought the Democratic Party was especially vulnerable. Pelosi's political cameo on the drag reality show came near the twilight of her career, but U.S. Representative Alexandra Ocasio-Cortez, of New York, leveraged the show to advance her progressive values as a freshmen congresswoman only just beginning to leave her mark on the national political stage (see **Case Study 4.2**).

Case Study 4.2   Alexandria Ocasio-Cortez judges drag

Figure 4.2 Alexandria Ocasio-Cortez participates as guest judge, with RuPaul and Carson Kressley, on an episode of *RuPaul's Drag Race*.

Source: Illustration by Eduardo Rangel.

Season 12 of *RuPaul's Drag Race* unveiled a lengthy list of celebrity guest judges, including Congresswoman Alexandria Ocasio-Cortez, often referred to as AOC. A passionate fan of the show, AOC appeared in a 2020 episode, offering words of encouragement and supportive feedback to contestants of the reality drag competition. The moment that stole the show came when contestant Jackie Cox shared that AOC's work gives them "hope for our country." An emotional Cox acknowledged the challenges their mother faced as an immigrant from Iran. The exchange was an opportunity for Ocasio-Cortez to reaffirm her commitment to inclusivity and humane immigration policies. Importantly, AOC seized on the opportunity to elaborate on the emotional exchange by making a surprise second cameo on *Untucked*, the show's backstage spin-off. There, AOC unveiled political narratives, reminding them that only a couple years ago she was bartending at a restaurant. The contestants were humbled by Ocasio-Cortez's presence and commended her on standing up to the president and standing up for her beliefs. AOC insisted that everyone effects change in their own way, artists and drag queens alike, adding, "And let's not forget who threw that first brick at Stonewall!" She is likely referring to drag queen Sylvia Rivera, a fierce advocate for the queer community and an integral part of the Stonewall riots, the protests that erupted in New York's Greenwich Village in response to police brutality against the LGBTQ community. The reference reinforced AOC's credibility with an important base of supporters for the progressive legislator. The cameo also allowed Ocasio-Cortez to champion inclusive values, unabashed support for marriage equality, and demonstrate her ability to connect with marginalized groups. The appearance bolstered her credibility with young voters and entertainment media like *Teen Vogue* and *People* covered the cameo and her reelection campaigns. Ocasio-Cortez easily won a second term in Congress in 2020, and a third term in 2022, increasing her already-wide margin of victory by 5 percentage points.

Far less common is the political cameo in Hollywood films. With a much longer and less predictable production timeline, cameos in films are more about increasing candidate exposure. Any lasting campaign effects would be far more indirect than television cameos that can be strategically timed in conjunction with key campaign events, critical primaries, and candidate announcements.

The star-studded rom-com *Wedding Crashers* featured a few D.C. heavyweights, including McCain. The 2005 cameo, in advance of his 2008 run for the White House, featured him alongside Democratic Party strategist James Carville in a scene where they congratulate two characters on the wedding of a prominent D.C. bride, the daughter of fictional U.S. Secretary William Cleary (Christopher Walken). The surprise hit, with a cast that included Owen Wilson, Rachel McAdams, and Vince Vaughn, drew several voters to the box office and netted close to $300 million. Just a couple of years earlier, another pop culture flick featured a soon-to-be presidential candidate.

New York Mayor Rudy Giuliani made a cameo in the 2003 slapstick comedy *Anger Management*, starring Adam Sandler and Jack Nicholson. Donning a Yankees jacket, Giuliani is a spectator at a Yankees game pleading with MLB officials to let Sandler's character remain in Yankee Stadium after they escort him from the field for disrupting the game. The punchline is that viewers watching the game on television at a bar misidentify Giuliani as talk show host Regis Philbin. And Bernie Sanders, then mayor of Burlington, Vermont, made a cameo in the relationship dramedy *Sweet Hearts Dance*. Sanders doles out candy to children trick-or-treating on Halloween night when a few hooligans drive by and egg his house. The 1988 release of the film coincided with Sanders' campaign for U.S. House of Representatives; although he lost the election that year, he ultimately would win the seat two years later.

But just how effective are such guest appearances across entertainment media? What measurable outcomes do cameos provide a campaign, if any? The benefits are likely to be more indirect and difficult to measure than other campaign strategies but that doesn't mean they are no less a priority in the contemporary campaign environment.

Assessing the campaign effectiveness of political cameos

Although political cameos are more prevalent in today's campaigns, political communication research lacks an understanding of their effectiveness. Television programs and films are often shot long before they air on television or release in the theaters, which makes it more difficult to utilize them strategically. Another wrench in the process comes from equal time laws, which may delay the release of an episode with a cameo until after an election if the opponent(s) were not provided with equal opportunity to appear. For example, CBS held a made-for-television movie featuring a cameo from President Clinton, who actively sought a second term in the White House, until after the 1996 election (L.A. Times Archives, 1996). Clinton's cameo in *A Child's Wish* centered on an ill teenager making a visit to the White House.

Despite the complications to taping schedules and equal time laws, political cameos humanize politicians and increase their relatability – attributes that matter to voters more in today's age of ubiquitous entertainment media. A well delivered can help to catapult a politician to become a prominent household name. The political cameo can essentially help a little-known politician become a pseudo celebrity of sorts, as we have seen with Arizona Senator John McCain. The cameos provide currency in the pop culture world and give politicians an opportunity to establish themselves as known and viable among a national audience. Repeated exposure to cameos may even yield **parasocial relationships** between voters and a candidate. These parasocial relationships are a psychological phenomenon in which researchers learned that consuming media could lead to imagined relationships and connections audience members feel toward mediated personas, entertainers, or even characters (Horton & Wohl, 1956). Heavy viewers of *The Apprentice* formed such parasocial connections to Trump, resulting in feeling more positive about the businessman and enabling them to dismiss negative news about him more easily (Gabriel et al., 2018). At the very least, Trump's lengthy resume of political cameos shows the power of sustained exposure in entertainment media.

Long before elected president in 2016, Donald Trump cultivated years of engagement with entertainment media, appearing in dozens of cameos. His first television cameo came in 1981 on *The Jeffersons* sitcom. The businessman and host of *The Apprentice* has since played himself in numerous television programs and Hollywood films, including *The Nanny*, *The Fresh Prince of Bel-Air*, *Sex and the City*, *Saturday Night Live*, *Home Alone 2*, *Little Rascals*, *Studio 54*, and *Zoolander*. The cameos all perpetuate the same narrative about Trump: a shrewd, wealthy, and uber successful businessman. These themes help to create the myth around the iconic real-estate mogul. Although not all his business ventures were successful and Trump was anything but a self-made man, the cameos worked in unison to establish the myth of his success. In fact, he even demanded television writers change up a script to introduce him as a billionaire rather than a millionaire (Rogers, 2016). Trump had zero experience in governing by the time he launched his 2016 campaign, but he had amassed more than 30 years of cameos across entertainment media, delivering his campaign instant name recognition and shaping public perception about his business acumen.

Trump's multiple cameos helped control the narratives about him and his success. Others utilize surprise appearances as a means of introducing themselves to a national audience, humanizing themselves to voters, or delivering brief policy points that affirm priorities and values.

One common method for humanizing a candidate is through gushing displays of fandom. McCain made headlines for expressing his fandom for *24*, as did Obama with his cameo on *MythBusters*. Biden also shared that he and his wife watch *Parks and Recreation*. New York mayor and presidential candidate Bill de Blasio cited his fandom for *The Simpsons* on more than one occasion before making his cameo on the show, and Ocasio-Cortez discussed the importance *Drag Race* played in her coming-home-from-work routines. These displays of fandom, often expressed in interviews, public appearances, and through social media accounts, demonstrate relatability, an every-person element to prominent politicians. For a voter to think "that candidate watches what *I* watch," or "they have good taste in shows," can make a politician seem more accessible and authentic. Another way cameos display humility is through the mistaken identity trope. This theme builds on the concept of self-deprecating humor by using the cameo as a punchline, that being the other characters in the scene have no idea that they are in the presence of a politician. Giuliani's cameo in *Anger Management* included a scene of bargoers misidentifying the mayor.

John Kerry's scene in *Cheers* featured two characters confusing the senator from their home state for a local news anchor. These cameos play down the ego the American public often associates with politicians while providing comedic relief. By being unafraid of being part of the punchline, the politicians appear more relatable.

Bolstering one's national profile and conveying a more relatable impression of the candidate are big parts of the cameo's purpose, but they can also function as a strategy to score policy points. Take Cory Booker's example of brining awareness to the incarceration among Blacks in *Being Mary Jane*. Bill Clinton's cameo in "A Child's Wish" enabled him to promote his 1993 signing of the Family and Medical Leave Act (L.A. Times Archives, 1996), which expanded leave for the birth of a child and for family medical emergencies. Even cameos in more comedic programs provide an opportunity to talk shop. Sanders plugged his economic policy priorities in an *SNL* sketch and Ocasio-Cortez reinforced the importance of the Marriage Equality Act on *Drag Race*.

In 2016, vice president and perpetual presidential candidate Joe Biden ignited a wave of social media buzz for his cameo on *Law & Order: SVU* (Jenkins, 2016) – an NBC crime drama that has thrived for more than 20 seasons. Unlike most cameos, Biden is awarded a significant script. Speaking to law enforcement, he expresses dismay over the backlog of untested rape kits across police departments nationwide, adding that it is a failure to women. Biden commends fictional Detective Olivia Benson (Mariska Hargitay) for her work on the issue of sexual assault before handing over the podium to her. In addition to the social media fury, the unusual appearance generated numerous headlines from national news organizations. The rapport Biden established with the cast and crew also led to indirect payoffs. Hargitay became a vocal supporter of Biden's 2020 campaign and spoke at the national convention.

Politicians may even deploy their spouses to make television cameos that help humanize them or keep national attention on specific policy goals. In 1983, Betty Ford appeared alongside her husband, President Gerald Ford, in an episode of *Dynasty* to raise awareness about childhood diabetes. First lady Nancy Reagan appeared on *Different Strokes* to tout the Reagan administration's "Just Say No" anti-drug campaign. Barbara Bush used *Sesame Street* as a platform to promote literacy, and the educational program has been a frequent stopping place for first ladies ever since. Hillary Clinton, Laura Bush, Michelle Obama, and Jill Biden all appeared in cameos on the PBS show.

The key to understanding the strategy of a political cameo is understanding that benefits are often indirect and difficult to measure. Working with celebrities can eventually lead to high level endorsements as it did for Biden. At minimum, political cameos generate considerable mainstream news attention and result in real time trending topics on social media – all while keeping a candidate top of mind to inattentive voters.

Summary

With the evolving role of cameos in the political campaign communication, we see yet another manifestation of the marriage between entertainment and politics. The increasing influence of these cameos and their ability to attract attention to a candidate and their campaign underscore how politicians have and continue to adapt to a media environment in which entertainment reigns supreme and news holds less influence over the electorate.

It is important to note that much has changed with the strategic use of political cameos. Cameos by politicians used to be sparse and not overly involved. But today most presidential candidates have made cameos in one or more entertainment programs and as more candidates engage, the scenes have become more participatory and involved. This means cameos are happening more frequently, lasting longer, and including more scripted responsibilities than ever before. Candidates must do more and say more to break through the abundance of media in the digital environment. All that rehearsing and canoodling with entertainers play a critically important role in building name recognition for candidates and conveying relatability to voters. These cameos are especially effective in humanizing big-name politicians and lesser-known candidates seeking longevity in public office; such appearances will cement their place in the national limelight, brokering memorable introductions to a mass audience.

Resources and references

Cramer Brownell, K. (2016, April 15). The Saturday night live episode that changed American politics. *Time*. https://time.com/4292027/gerald-ford-saturday-night-live/

Daugherty, G. (2018, May 16). Did Nixon's "laugh-in" cameo help him win the 1968 election? *History.com*. www.history.com/news/richard-nixon-laugh-in-cameo-1968

Dugan, A. (2018, August 26). John McCain well-known, well-liked for much of his career. *Gallup*. https://news.gallup.com/opinion/gallup/237764/john-mccain-known-liked-career.aspx

Foggatt, T. (2019, September 23). The art of the political cameo. *The New Yorker*. www.new-yorker.com/magazine/2019/09/30/the-2020-presidential-race-as-told-through-cameos

Gabriel, S., Paravati, E., Green, M. C., & Flomsbee, J. (2018). From apprentice to president: The role of parasocial connection in the election of Donald Trump. *Social Psychological and Personality Science, 9*(3), 299–307.

Horton, D., & Wohl, R. R. (1956). Mass communication and para-social interaction. *Psychiatry, 19*(3), 215–229.

Jenkins, N. (2016, September 29). Joe Biden appeared on law and order: SVU and the internet loved it. *Time*. https://time.com/4512621/joe-biden-law-and-order-rape-kits/

L.A. Times Archives. (1996, May 5). Clinton to appear in TV movie that touts family leave law. *Los Angeles Times*. www.latimes.com/archives/la-xpm-1996-05-05-mn-810-story.html

NBC. (2021, January 21). *Joe Biden pays his friend Benson a visit – law & order: SVU* [Video]. NBC.com. www.nbc.com/law-and-order-special-victims-unit/video/joe-biden-pays-his-friend-benson-a-visit-law-order-svu/4307063

Patterson, T. (2006, February 7). Senator, we're ready for your cameo: What was John McCain doing on 24? *Slate*. https://slate.com/culture/2006/02/john-mccain-on-24.html

Rogers, K. (2016, October 26). How Donald Trump used Hollywood to create "Donald Trump". *The New York Times*. www.nytimes.com/2016/10/27/business/media/donald-trump-movies-tv-cameos.html

RuPaul's Drag Race [RuPaul's Drag Race]. (2020, December 6). *AOC joins the queens in untucked* [Video]. YouTube. www.youtube.com/watch?v=cDT_M89OeBU

Saturday Night Live. (2001, September 29). *9/11 tribute with Mayor Rudy Giuliani* [Video]. NBC.com/Saturday Night Live. www.nbc.com/saturday-night-live/video/911-tribute-with-mayor-giuliani/2750172

St. James, E., & Framke, C. (2015, November 8). Donald Trump's Saturday night live episode was worse than bad – it was boring. *Vox*. www.vox.com/culture/2015/11/8/9690978/saturday-night-live-donald-trump

Waxman, S. (1996, February 7). Murphy Brown's soft spot sitcom goes easy on guest Newt Gingrich. *The Washington Post*. www.washingtonpost.com/archive/lifestyle/1996/02/07/murphy-browns-soft-spot-sitcom-goes-easy-on-guest-newt-gingrich/d1f5ff32-6a5a-45f0-81f6-b9d5519dd255/

5 Partnerships in pop culture

Courting the celebrity endorsement

Think for a minute about the biggest celebrity you met. Did you get an auto-graph? Or perhaps you scored backstage passes to one of your favorite musical acts. Regardless of where it happened, the caliber of the celebrity, or the cir-cumstances, you were likely compelled to share the experience with your fam-ily and friends or humble brag to your social media followers: #blessed #lucky. Such reactions are expected in a culture that puts celebrity on a pedestal. And in the digital age, such encounters become publicly shared experiences that can also elevate our own stature. This phenomenon is no different when a politician aligns themselves with celebrities.

The influence of celebrities on campaign fundraising is not novel to the contemporary media environment; however, celebrity influence is more vis-ible in today's age of media abundance. Moreover, celebrities are increasingly playing a far more active role in the campaign process – a role that goes far beyond fundraising. From convention speeches and rally appearances to live performances, and video endorsements published on social media, this chapter explores the expanding role celebrities play in the campaign process and exam-ines the ways candidates court celebrity influence.

The evolution of celebrity endorsers

Merely listing all the celebrity endorsements of presidential candidates over recent election cycles would exceed the allowable word count for this text. Here's a small slice from the 2020 election:

The 2020 general election included a slew of celebrity endorsements for the Biden-Harris ticket including John Legend, Eva Longoria, Mindy Kaling, Leonardo DiCaprio, Chris Evans, Harry Styles, Brad Pitt, Selena Gomez, Lizzo, Beyonce, Miley Cyrus, Mariah Carey, Cardi B, Justin Timberlake, Jennifer Lawrence, Taylor Swift, Jennifer Lopez, Alex Rodriguez, Billie Eilish, Lin-Manuel Miranda, and Tom Hanks. Celebrities supporting Trump included Brett Farve, Stacey Dash, 50 Cent, Jon Voight, Kid Rock, Lil' Wayne, and Kanye or "Ye" West (before officially launching his own presidential campaign). The list gets lengthier when accounting for endorsements made during the primaries.

DOI: 10.4324/9781003364832-5

Dave Chappelle, Elon Musk, and Donald Glover endorsed Andrew Yang; Cardi B and Ariana Grande endorsed Bernie Sanders; Clint Eastwood endorsed Michael Bloomberg; and Pete Buttigieg drew endorsements from Gwyneth Paltrow, George Takei, and Ellen DeGeneres.

Prior to John F. Kennedy's 1960 presidential campaign, celebrity support for candidates was limited and often remained behind the scenes, out of the public spotlight. Entertainers Al Jolson and Mary Pickford were some of the earliest examples of celebrity involvement in U.S. presidential politics; however, historians note that their involvement was commercial rather than political and they were financially compensated for working on spot ads for Warren Harding's 1920 campaign (Harvey, 2018). In the early part of the 20th century, entertainers avoided politics, which was often seen as a commercial risk. Moreover, active engagement in political campaigns could breach contracts talent had with their respective studios (Harvey, 2018). By the 1930s and 1940s, radio's golden age, some talent began to support politicians. Franklin D. Roosevelt quietly drew support from actors Mickey Rooney and Lucille Ball. Dwight Eisenhower hired actors Robert Montgomery and George Murphy to help delivery of messaging and advertising concepts (Cramer Brownell, 2014). By 1960, celebrities exuded more influence over public life thanks to television and commercial advertising. And Kennedy's comfort level with television and family connections helped him establish a rapport with Hollywood.

Kennedy's access was boosted by his father's background as a former film studio executive and the acting career of his brother-in-law, Peter Lawford, who would help the candidate build a network of Hollywood endorsements that increased voter turnout (Cramer Brownell, 2014). Kennedy was adept at attracting support from prominent entertainers. Nat King Cole, Judy Garland, and Harry Belafonte endorsed Kennedy. The group of performers known as The Rat Pack (Frank Sinatra, Dean Martin, Sammy Davis Jr., Joey Bishop, and Peter Lawford) were coined "The Jack Pack" for their public support of Kennedy. Sinatra would even repurpose his song "High Hopes" to later be used at campaign events. Sinatra's active campaigning would also foreshadow the expanding role celebrities would later play in electoral politics.

Between 1960 and 2000, celebrity endorsements for political candidates were not unheard of but somewhat sporadic. Nixon attracted endorsements from John Wayne and basketball great Wilt Chamberlain. The 1980 Democratic primaries prompted celebrity endorsements for Jimmy Carter, Massachusetts Senator Ted Kennedy, and California Governor Jerry Brown. Of course, Reagan, a Hollywood heavyweight, attracted a host of celebrity supporters in the general election. Although the importance of a celebrity checkbook and their influence on public opinion existed as early as radio's golden age, once the intersection between entertainment and politics fully integrated in today's era of media abundance, the volume of endorsements accelerated with tremendous speed and celebrities adopted a more active role in the campaign process.

For example, actress Gabrielle Union not only endorsed Obama for his 2008 and 2012 campaigns but also appeared at campaign events. Union worked alongside the reelection campaign's "Greater Together" initiative designed to engage young voters across Historically Black Colleges and Universities. When endorsing Michael Bloomberg's 2020 presidential campaign, television's Judge Judy appeared on news outlets and talk show circuits to campaign on his behalf. The judge granted interviews with *CNN, People, The View, Real Time with Bill Maher*, and penned a 2019 op-ed for *USA Today* that endorsed Bloomberg before he officially announced his campaign. Guitarist Ted Nugent not only performed at Trump rallies but also hosted live streamed virtual "spirit campfires" providing behind the scenes access to campaign events.

A celebrity in the age of social media no longer quietly writes a check and supports candidates behind the scenes. They use a host of digital platforms, mainstream media, and even campaign tactics to publicly advocate for candidates. In the age of the media's long tail, celebrities are even expected to weigh in on divisive social and political issues – elections included.

Merriam-Webster defines **celebrity** as the "state of being celebrated: fame." Celebrity is a certain level of status or notoriety affixed to an individual and could not exist without mass media. Celebrity was once associated with accomplishments, talent, and skills but reality television democratized fame, expanding stardom to ordinary people who appear more like us. Reality television made real-estate agents, fitness gurus, interior designers, chefs, and game show contestants pseudo-celebrities. Social media expanded our notion of celebrity even further as anyone with looks, opinions, or a following can achieve fame in online influencer culture. Celebrities are considered newsworthy because of their **prominence** or the state of being distinct, important, or notable. Prominence is part of the criteria that news professionals use to judge what is newsworthy. When campaigns partner with celebrities, it all but guarantees a media spectacle and headlines for the candidate (Payne et al., 2007). There are a variety of ways campaigns can achieve spectacle through partnerships with celebrities, one of the earliest being the party conventions.

The national conventions: a who's who of "A" listers

One of the longstanding platforms for engaging celebrity endorsers has been through an invitation to **party conventions**, which are held during the summer months after state primaries and caucuses when the Republican and Democratic parties have winnowed down their respective nominee. These conventions formally allow delegates from each state to select the party nominee while also establishing an agenda for the general election campaign. Celebrities are increasingly integrated into the multiday convention schedules.

In 2008, Daddy Yankee, Jon Voight, Robert Downey, Jr., and Ben Stein appeared at the Republican Convention in support of John McCain. Ben Affleck, Oprah Winfrey, Susan Sarandon, Kanye West, John Legend, and Jennifer Lopez were among the stars rallying for Obama at the Democratic Convention. The 2012 Republican National Convention featured a rambling speech from film legend Clint Eastwood (see **Case Study 5.1**). In 2016, a slew of prominent

Case Study 5.1   Clint Eastwood spitballs to an empty chair at RNC

Figure 5.1 Clint Eastwood steals the spotlight from presidential candidate Mitt Romney, with an unusual performative speech at the Republican National Convention.

Source: Illustration by Eduardo Rangel.

Hollywood juggernaut Clint Eastwood is known for playing rough and tumble characters on the big screen, has a long history of supporting conservative candidates, and was even considered as a potential running mate for George H. W. Bush. Bush wasn't the first or last to court Eastwood's influence. Mitt Romney sought Eastwood's endorsement in the 2012 election and after the actor spoke at a campaign fundraising event in Idaho, the Romney campaign invited the 82-year-old actor to appear at the Republican National Convention as a surprise speaker. Eastwood's speech, reportedly unvetted by the campaign and largely ad-libbed, quickly became an unmitigated disaster (Brooks, 2013). The speech centered on a hypothetical conversation he was acting out with an imaginary President Obama, represented by an empty high-top chair. Eastwood portrayed both himself and the president during the performance, intended to be a critique of Obama's first term. Eastwood called imaginary Obama "crazy" and abruptly blurted, "I'm not going to shut up; it's my turn!" to the empty chair. The performative speech drew some laughs from the crowd but didn't sit well with most viewers at home and the backlash across social media and mainstream media was swift and merciless (Lee, 2012; Abdullah, 2012). In real time, parodies and memes unfolded with "invisibleObama" and "Eastwooding" – a verb to describe people talking to empty chairs – trending on Twitter. Political analysts called the moment "a national punchline" (Abdullah, 2012). Stuart Stevens, a campaign strategist for Romney reportedly excused himself to vomit during the speech (Brooks, 2013). The performative speech was so bizarre, that it was the aspect of the convention generating the most news. Romney's speech and national moment was overshadowed by Eastwood's meltdown, as the actor – not the candidate – dominated the headlines. Moreover, the content of Eastwood's speech was so preoccupied with Obama that there was little advocacy for the Romney-Ryan ticket. Instead of a big celebrity endorsement, the surprise Eastwood's speech underscored the dangers of aligning with larger-than-life celebrities capable of stealing the show.

women spoke on behalf of the first woman to win a party's nomination: Hillary Clinton. Sarah Silverman, Eva Longoria, America Ferrera, and Elizabeth Banks were on the docket for the Democratic National Convention. Even digital celebrities known merely for their ability to persuade online followers to support products and brands, or what we collectively refer to as **influencers**, began playing an active role in the 2016 conventions, after YouTube star and beauty vlogger Elle Walker spoke at the Democratic National Convention. Celebrities are typically deployed at these events for one of three purposes: issues-based advocacy that helps advance the party's agenda; emphasizing character appeals for the candidate; or performance and entertainment value.

In May 1995, *Superman* actor Christopher Reeve suffered a horrific horse-riding accident that broke his neck and ultimately paralyzed him from the shoulders down. One year later, he spoke at the 1996 Democratic Convention in support of a Clinton-Gore reelection. Ushered out on a wheelchair and ventilator, Reeve pled for more funding for stem cell research. He personalized his experience with the spinal cord injury to suggest that the Clinton-Gore ticket would do more for advances in healthcare and medicine. Similarly, reality television star and co-host from *The View* Elizabeth Hasselbeck entered the stage at the 2004 Republican Convention, sharing her mother's breast cancer battle – a cancer that has ravaged several of Hasselbeck's family members. Through personalized issues-based advocacy, Hasselbeck was unequivocal in her support for President George W. Bush, citing "aggressive research" under his leadership. Actress Scarlett Johansson also spoke about healthcare during the 2012 Democratic Convention, advocating for Obama's reelection by sharing personal narratives of her family's struggle to pay for medical bills. Her speech reinforced the party's issue agenda of strengthening Medicaid and preserving Planned Parenthood. More recently, *Law & Order: SVU* star Mariska Hargitay delivered a 2020 Democratic Convention speech – a virtual speech due to the COVID-19 pandemic. Hargitay spoke of her nonprofit, the Joyful Heart Foundation, an organization working on issues related to sexual assault, child welfare, and domestic violence. Her appearance acted as a continuation of issues raised during Biden's 2016 *SVU* cameo in which the two raised awareness of a national backlog of untested rape kits.

The convention endorsement from a celebrity can highlight issue strengths of a candidate. These examples of issues-based advocacy rely on personal narratives and storytelling, and celebrities also help establish character appeals.

For example, actor Tommy Lee Jones visited the 2000 Democratic Convention to guide delegates through a trip down memory lane. Jones, Al Gore's college roommate at Harvard University, shared personal anecdotes, including memories of shooting pool, hunting trips in Tennessee and the roommates' fandom for Star Trek. The speech centered on Gore's character and kindness. Celebrity couple Angie Harmon, actress from *Law & Order*, and the NFL's Jason Sehorn, co-delivered a speech at the 2004 Republican Convention to share political narratives, focused on the story of Medal of Honor recipient Rudy P. Hernandez and his heroics while serving in the Korean War. The narrative was used to portray Bush as a pro-military candidate who understands the values of honor, service, and duty. *Scandal* actress Kerry Washington appealed to Obama's character by also evoking personal narratives that alluded to shared values. Washington shared her experience as the daughter of an immigrant; she celebrated the nation's diversity and Obama's commitment to that diversity.

These character appeals serve as another mechanism for humanizing candidates and act as testimonials from prominent figures that may be perceived as more trustworthy than political elites. These prominent celebrities can also use their talents to fire up the base and set the tone of a convention through performance.

Alicia Keys, a performer at the 2016 Democratic Convention, dedicated songs "Superwoman" and "In Common" to mothers who lost children to violence and the unification of Clinton and Sanders supporters. Other musical acts have not only performed but also written original tunes to advance the endorsed candidate. John Rich amped up the Republican Convention in 2008 by performing his original song for the campaign: "Raisin' McCain." The up-tempo country tune energized the party base, with Rich's ultimatum-like refrain "You can get on the train or get out of the way, we're all just raisin' McCain!" For the virtual lineup of the 2020 Democratic Convention, young artist Billie Eilish urged the audience to vote, stressing the urgency of social justice and climate change, before debuting her song "My Future" for the convention.

Another longstanding partnership between candidates and celebrities centers on campaign fundraising. And these once private events have attracted much more visibility in the era of social media and the competitive news landscape that prioritizes entertainment content.

Fundraisers and "red carpet" galas

Barack Obama's first presidential campaign notably had Oprah Winfrey in its pocket as a strong endorser. Oprah's influence went beyond endorsement by lending her celebrity and network to fundraise for the campaign. Oprah hosted a grand fundraiser in her Malibu home for the 2008 campaign and over the course of his two campaigns, her fundraisers secured more than a few million for Obama (Kornhaber, 2016). In 2012 "Queen Bey" Beyonce and her husband, rapper Jay-Z, cohosted an Obama campaign fundraiser at Jay-Z's 40/40 club, where the candidate made a special appearance. That event pulled in approximately $4 million for the campaign and a fundraiser later hosted by George Clooney totaled $15 million for Obama (Bradshaw, 2012). With fundraising momentum being one predictor of electoral success, particularly early fundraising momentum, campaigns continually look to celebrities and their extensive networks to raise cash.

The fundraising collaborations build a war chest for campaigns that are getting increasingly expensive. They also grant celebrities the opportunity to expand their influence beyond entertainment circles. A 2004 Beverly Hills gala hosted by businessman Ron Burkle attracted Jennifer Aniston, Brad Pitt, Leonardo DiCaprio, and dozens of others to support Democratic candidate John Kerry. The event netted approximately $6 million for the Kerry campaign; attendees had the opportunity to hobnob with a potential future president. The gala fetched $1,000 per ticket, with additional donations encouraged. According to reports, the higher the donation, the more access it landed the celebrity, with the highest donors welcomed to an exclusive private reception with Kerry (Glaister & Borger, 2004). George Clooney helped raise millions for Hillary Clinton in 2016. One gala hosted by George and Amal Clooney was reportedly priced north of $33,000 a person, and the event drew Ellen DeGeneres, Jane Fonda, and Jim Parsons. Another 2016 Clinton event charged guests more than $350,000 to be tabled with Clooney, and others promised guests the chance to mingle with Justin Timberlake, Eva Longoria, Steven Spielberg, and other mystery celebrity guests (Wright, 2020).

Democratic presidential candidates have an especially lengthy list of celebrity partnerships, partly a reflection of Hollywood politics being more aligned with the more liberal leaning ideology of the party. Bill Clinton's embrace of entertainment media in the 1992 campaign also helped strengthen the bonds between the Democratic Party and Hollywood (Kettle, 2000). That isn't to say Republican candidates skip the celebrity courting altogether. John McCain's 2008 campaign attracted endorsements and financial support from Sylvester

Stallone and Kelsey Grammar, and Mitt Romney drew support from Eastwood and Chuck Norris. Romney, now a vocal critic of Trump, even sought out Trump's endorsement in 2012. A Trump-hosted April 2012 fundraiser in New York attracted more than 400 guests at $50,000 ticket, helping Romney secure the nomination (Wright, 2020).

Exclusive fundraising events help to cultivate long-lasting relationships with celebrities, guaranteeing subsequent political donations from prominent people and their extensive networks. Influence begets influence. Celebrity appearances at galas and high-profile donations help a campaign build momentum, attracting attention from other elites with deep pockets. But in today's campaign environment, candidates are courting celebrities for more than just cash; they also use their art to communicate values and relate to voters.

Campaigns find the right tone with musical partnerships

From concert rallies, campaign jams, and the curating of playlists, commercial music is playing an especially prominent role in political campaign communication. Music can signal to voters a candidate's values and convey relatability. Contemporary campaigns are routinely leveraging commercial music to engage voters, raise funds, and establish a tone.

In 1980, country singers Willie Nelson, Loretta Lynn, and Johnny Cash held concerts to support Southern Democrat Jimmy Carter, but by 2016, campaign involvement from commercial musicians expanded considerably, appealing to a variety of genres and fan bases. Kid Rock, Wayne Newton, and Ted Nugent performed on the campaign trail for Trump. Clinton, on the other hand, leveraged pop music acts to perform across swing states ahead of the election. Calling the performances "Love Trumps Hate," the Clinton campaign hosted Jay-Z for a performance in Cleveland, Ohio, and Katy Perry performed in Philadelphia, Pennsylvania – two critical swing states for candidates (Coscarelli, 2016). The 2020 presidential election included partnerships with a lengthy list of musical acts. During the Democratic primaries, Bon Iver, Vampire Weekend, and The Strokes were featured at concert rallies in support of Bernie Sanders. In the general election, Kid Rock hosted a September rock rally for Trump in the musician's home state of Michigan and John Legend performed at a 2020 drive-in event for the Biden-Harris ticket. And these partnerships are no longer limited to the performer entering the political domain; sometimes, it's the candidate infiltrating the performative space.

At the 2022 Austin City Limits music festival at Texas, gubernatorial candidate Beto O'Rourke surprised the crowd with Kacey Musgraves. During the singer–songwriter's headlining set, Musgraves asked, "Honestly, I could use a drink. Is there any beer or anything out there?" – O'Rourke's cue to scurry on stage to hand the singer a beer. The joint appearance ignited a roaring applause from the crowd. His time campaigning at ACL was well spent, with endorsements coming from other headlining acts including The Chicks, Willie Nelson, and lead singer of the band Paramore (Aniftos, 2022). Despite O'Rourke's rock star appeal, endorsements have not guaranteed his electoral success, but the spectacle may have helped the liberal candidate expand the influence of the Democratic Party in a historically conservative state.

Live performances are just one method of bringing commercial music into the campaign fold. Campaigns appropriate mainstream music in a variety of ways to energize voters, communicate values, and demonstrate relatability. Commercial music is a considerable component of the contemporary campaign event. Baseball fans are likely familiar with the concept of a walk-up song, an energizing representation of the batter that's played when it's their turn at the plate. The song has a dual purpose of showcasing the roots, personality, or values of the player while motivating them and amping up the crowd. The "campaign jam" operates no differently. The song is played at rallies, key campaign events, and inaugurations, becoming symbolic of the values a candidate stands for and sometimes operating as a *perceived* endorsement from the musician.

Candidates initially tapped artists to repurpose old hits or pen original tunes for their campaigns or they might select wildly patriotic tunes such as Lee Greenwood's "God Bless the U.S.A." as Ronald Reagan's chose for his 1984 campaign jam. True to his embracing of entertainment media, Bill Clinton was drawn to a mainstream rock track: Fleetwood Mac's "Don't Stop (Thinking about Tomorrow)." This would foreshadow the expanding role rock-pop music would play in political campaign communication. More recent campaign jams include Hillary Clinton's use of Katy Perry's "Roar" and Trump's use of Pharrell's "Happy." Mitt Romney loaded up on the patriotic appeals with Kid Rock's "Born Free." And Pete Buttigieg embraced his relative youth with an alt rock favorite, Panic! at the Disco's "High Hopes."

An effective campaign jam features the following characteristics: a hopeful tone, up-tempo pace, patriotic, pastoral, or inclusive lyrics, and a universally recognized artist void of major controversy. An effective campaign jam should also have the artist's blessing. Without their approval, appropriating a musician's work for campaign purposes can result in legal entanglements, social media backlash, or the artist actively campaigning against the candidate. This predicament has been more common for Republican candidates, many of whom find less support among prominent musical artists relative to their Democratic opponents. Using a celebrity's work for campaign purposes gives the illusion of an endorsement, and that has irked some artists. Phil Collins, The Rolling Stones, Neil Young, and Queen were among the artists outraged over Trump's use of their music at campaign events (Behr, 2020). Trump faced a legal cease-and-desist battle from the Village People for using "Y.M.C.A." as a campaign jam and George W. Bush faced legal threats from Tom Petty for using his hit song "I won't back down."

The candidates are not only engaging in commercial music for campaign jams but also showcasing their musical tastes by sharing eclectic playlists with prospective voters. Nothing humanizes a candidate quite like their ability to curate a hip Spotify playlist. Obama was the first candidate (and first-sitting president) to publish his playlists. His "2012 Campaign Playlist" on Spotify, unveiled through the president's official Twitter account, featured hits from Earth, Wind and Fire, No Doubt, U2, Aretha Franklin, and Arcade Fire. The novelty of the presidential playlist also inspired the plot of a Season 2 episode of HBO's *Veep*. In the episode "Running," VP Selina Myer (Julia Louis-Dreyfus) frantically mobilizes her staff to release a playlist after her opponent publishes one. Obama normalized this method of relating to the electorate by continuing to publish official White House playlists on Spotify. By the 2020 campaign, a playlist was all but expected of the presidential candidates. Andrew Yang, Kamala Harris, Beto O'Rourke, Elizabeth Warren, Bernie Sanders, Kirsten Gillibrand, Cory Booker, Julian Castro, Joe Biden, and Donald Trump all released playlists during the campaign.

Playlists are not only a means of conveying values and humanizing the candidates but also about connecting with specific subsets of voters. Thus, selecting songs isn't so simple, and strategy guides the careful curation of the campaign playlist. Some select artists that reflect the diversity of the electorate. According to Herndon's (2019) analysis of campaign music, Harris selected a list of nearly all Black and Latino artists, critical voting groups for the Democratic Party; Warren selected songs with working class themes, in line with her populist platforms; and Gillibrand, who centered her campaign on women's issues such as family leave and abortion, mainly selected female artists. Some candidates strive for authenticity, curating a playlist that reflects their identity and roots. For example, Castro was the only candidate to include Spanish language tracks, whereas O'Rourke, who once performed in a punk rock band, filled his playlist with rock tunes. Some candidates also consider inclusion: Castro's playlist was evenly split between male and female artists, whereas Biden's had equal representation from Black and white artists.

Campaigns are also tapping into the creativity of artists to develop music video endorsements. Eminem created an original video for rap anthem "Lose Yourself" for the Biden-Harris campaign, re-editing to feature montages of the candidates. Both Eminem and Biden shared the video on their respective YouTube accounts on November 2, fetching more than 1 million views. Jay-Z worked with Obama's 2012 campaign to create a video encouraging young people to register and vote. The video, which drew parallels between the president and the rapper, was shared by Jay-Z at the "Made in America" music festival and on Obama's official YouTube account. Earlier, in 2008, another artist supporting Obama would ultimately reimagine the concept of celebrity endorsements, taking them to the digital age. Will.i.am, former member of Black Eyed Peas, would create a video mashup to an Obama campaign speech that featured more than two dozen celebrities spanning music, film, and television (see **Case Study 5.2**).

Case Study 5.2 will.i.am summons celebs for Obama

Figure 5.2 Featuring more than 20 celebrities, musical artist will.i.am. creates a buzzworthy video endorsement for Barack Obama's 2008 campaign.

Source: Illustration by Eduardo Rangel.

Disappointed after an unsuccessful endorsement of Democrat John Kerry in 2004, Black Eyed Peas singer will.i.am moved beyond a band performance when the time came to endorse Obama in 2008. This time he built a coalition of celebrity support in a 4:30-minute video in the form of song. He summoned more than two dozen celebrities to mobilize for the candidate, including Scarlett Johansson, Kareem Abdul-Jabbar, Common, John Legend, Nicole Scherzinger, and Nick Cannon. The mashup of Obama's New Hampshire speech (written by speechwriter Jon Favreau) featured celebrity endorsers singing, humming, and echoing the candidate's words in a moving cadence as black and white footage of Obama was juxtaposed with reel of the celebrity collaborators. The slate of endorsers was diverse and appeared genuinely inspired by the candidate. The mashup was so novel and featured so many entertainers that it erupted through the white noise of the web, generating colossal mainstream news attention. Within three weeks of publishing the video on Dipdive and YouTube, will.i.am's project garnered more than 25 million views (Wallsten, 2010). The Obama campaign quickly embraced the video, posting it on its official blog and campaign website. John Legend and will.i.am. were invited to perform "Yes We Can" at the national convention. The speech set to song reinforced the campaign's theme of hope, alluding to women's rights, inclusion, equality, opportunity, and progress – values that excite the Democratic base. The success of the viral endorsement video bolstered enthusiasm for Obama, a challenger to the better-known frontrunner: Hillary Clinton. Despite the loss in the New Hampshire primary, the underdog candidate that trailed Clinton by double digits through December 2007, bounced back on Super Tuesday, held just three days after the video endorsement dropped (Carroll, 2007). Obama won 13 Super Tuesday states relative to Clinton's 8 and gained more pledged delegates than the frontrunner. By February 2008, analysts and pollsters were beginning to call the race a tossup.

Online and social media: the public nature of today's endorsements

Following that star-studded will.i.am. endorsement, celebrities are throwing their support for candidates in droves and doing so by publishing social media posts and digital videos that circulate online platforms, go viral, and generate news attention for both the celebrity and the candidate.

Golfer Jack Nicklaus helped make headlines for Trump's 2020 reelection campaign. Using his personal Twitter account, the Ohio native's endorsement appealed to middle-class Midwestern values and the American Dream. Actor Jon Voight's tweet in support of Trump featured a video published in September 2020. Dressed formally, with the U.S. flag as his backdrop, Voight calmly cautioned against liberal thinkers and evoked biblical metaphors to advocate support for Trump's reelection. Voight insisted that the election was an opportunity for America to "renews vows" with God. All kinds of celebrities took to their social media accounts during the 2020 Democratic primaries to throw their weight behind a candidate. Comedian Dave Chappelle and tech mogul Elon Musk announced their endorsements for Andrew Yang through their Twitter accounts. Selena Gomez used Instagram to share her 2020 endorsement for Kamala Harris. Soccer star Megan Rapinoe added an extra personal touch to her social-media endorsement of Elizabeth Warren.

Rapinoe posted a recorded phone conversation between her and Warren. When Warren calls Rapinoe, they share a few laughs and share their concerns about inequality in America. Rapinoe proudly states "consider me Team Warren" before the call ends. The conversation is emblematic of a newer trend in which celebrity endorsements no longer happen in a vacuum and celebrities are increasingly sharing rehearsed exchanges and interactions with the candidates.

Doing so enhances the credibility of the endorser, suggesting to voters that they are properly vetting the candidates they support while allowing a little more campaign control over the messaging. For example, rapper Cardi B and Bernie Sanders met at the TEN Nail Bar, a salon in Detroit, where she asked the presidential candidate a list of questions addressing issues that matter to her and her fans. She concluded the recorded 12-minute talk with an appeal to her followers: "Let's feel the Bern!" The 2019 video endorsement was uploaded to the star's social media and Sanders' official campaign accounts, drawing a YouTube audience of more than 1.25 million viewers.

The latest iteration of the video endorsement has celebrities taking a more active role in the campaign process. With interview-style videos, celebrities essentially supplant the role that was once reserved for journalists. These celebrity collaborations iron out a brief list of issues to draw attention to and highlight character strengths. Biden's 2020 campaign deployed this strategy with help from Dwayne "The Rock" Johnson, Jennifer Lopez, and Alex Rodriguez.

In a virtual conversation with both Biden and Harris, Johnson led an interview-style endorsement. The wrestler-turned actor used the video to talk up the compassion and credentials of the candidates, adding that Harris is "a certified badass." The 2020 video attracted close to half a million views on YouTube. That same year, Biden's campaign arranged an interview-style endorsement with actress/singer Jennifer Lopez and her then fiancé Alex Rodriguez, retired baseball player. Joe and Jill Biden appeared on camera opposite the power couple. The Bidens spoke with them about racial injustice and their shared faith. Lopez advocated for issues relevant to the Latino community, stressing that many had put their lives at risk to work during dangerous pandemic conditions. The celebrity appeals emphasized race and faith and delivered endorsements in both English and Spanish, enhancing Biden's credibility with Latino voters. Biden's campaign also arranged a question-and-answer segment on Instagram Live with influencer Bethany Mota, allowing the candidate a platform for reaching 4.7 million followers.

Celebrity endorsements aren't always born from political motivations, and new digital tools enable campaigns to even seek involvement from celebrities looking to financially capitalize on their name, likeness, and image. The increasing demand for video content has brought some campaigns to Cameo, an online platform where celebrities create customized videos for fees ranging from $1–25,000. Originally conceived as a way for fans to pay celebrities to deliver motivating messages, birthday greetings, or congratulations on a milestone, now Cameo is emerging as a tool for paid political endorsements.

Republican congressional candidate Greg Raths' 2020 campaign reportedly used Cameo to pay celebrity Fox News pundit Tomi Lahren for a 30-second campaign video (Staggs, 2020). Although Lahren and Raths never formally met, Raths used the video as a Lahren endorsement on his campaign social media. Democrats have dabbled with Cameo, too. Pennsylvania U.S. Senate candidate John Fetterman partnered with *Jersey Shore*'s Snookie for video content in 2022. The attack ad featured Snookie drawing attention to opponent Mehmet Oz's abrupt move from New Jersey to Pennsylvania, suggesting that he relocated for strategic purposes and could not fully understand the needs of the constituency he would be representing in the Senate. According to a Fetterman campaign spokesperson, the Cameo platform was on brand for the laid-back candidate, a prolific Twitter user, and hooded sweatshirt aficionado; Snookie received $400 in compensation (Cioffi, 2022).

In 2014, Joe Biden foreshadowed his presidential campaign with a video partnership with Julia Luis-Dreyfus – who later became a vocal supporter of Biden's 2020 campaign – and HBO, parodying the show *Veep* while making light of their presidential ambitions. The video, which includes cameos from Nancy Pelosi and Michelle Obama, concludes with Biden and Dreyfus's character VP Selina Meyer getting "45" tattooed to their wrists. Campaigns and celebrities continue to chart new waters with video endorsements, tinkering with style, format, and the level of creative output from the entertainer.

The NBA's Steph Curry created a video endorsement for Biden and Harris in 2022, engaging his entire family in the process. Curry was joined by his wife Ayesha and their two daughters where, as a family, they spoke about social justice, inequality, and the environment. They encouraged their young daughters to join the conversation, asking them about the importance of a woman vice president. Justin Timberlake's endorsement of the ticket came in the form of a surprise appearance in a video conference, applauding a team of young phone bank volunteers working in Pennsylvania, a key swing state in the general election. Sharing his face time with the volunteers and his Biden endorsement on Instagram, the video attracted more than 1.6 million views. And two video endorsements made in 2022 from actress Gwyneth Paltrow and Snoop Dogg weren't for a high-profile national race but were published online to support the campaign of a political outsider running for mayor of Los Angeles.

State-level races attract star power

The extent of celebrity influence permeates all levels of electoral politics in a media environment in which entertainment reigns supreme. Candidate-celebrity partnerships are now a fixture for state-level races and may even influence local electoral politics.

For example, Democratic frontrunner in the 2022 Los Angeles mayoral race, Karen Bass, saw her polling lead quickly dwindle after high-profile celebrities took to digital media to weigh in on the race. Her opponent, businessman Rick Caruso, narrowed the polling gap following endorsements from Gwyneth Paltrow, Snoop Dogg, George Lopez, Kim Kardashian, and Katy Perry (Noah, 2022). And appearing alongside the candidate during campaign events, Jane Fonda endorsed Kenneth Mejia, the outsider progressive candidate who was elected Los Angeles City Controller in 2021. And celebrities are lending support to a variety of candidates in state-level races.

Two Democrats received somewhat surprising endorsements from Taylor Swift during the 2018 U.S. midterm elections. Swift, who remained politically neutral for much of her career, posted an Instagram endorsement for Democratic U.S. Senate candidate Phil Bredesen and Jim Cooper for the U.S. House of Representatives running in her home state of Tennessee. Her endorsement was credited with boosting statewide voter registration figures and her decision to enter the political fray was the subject of a Netflix documentary *Miss Americana*. O'Rourke received celebrity support in bids for the U.S. Senate and later his gubernatorial campaign, including from Houston-native Beyonce. In 2020, comedian and actor Kumail Najiani endorsed Jon Ossoff in the Georgia U.S. Senate race, conducting an Instagram Live chat with the candidate, and Jennifer Lawrence endorsed Democrat Amy McGrath in her home state of Kentucky.

In today's era of the media's long tail, no level of office is immune to celebrity influence. Celebrities are expanding their electoral influence across national, state, and even local races and touting their support in the highly public domain of social media. But how meaningful are such endorsements?

Assessing the campaign effectiveness of courting celebrities

Marketing research has shown that celebrity endorsements of commercial products boost company sales on average of 4% (Elberse & Verleun, 2012). Even with the commodification of campaigns, candidates are not technically commercial goods, but what if we applied this finding to political "brands," meaning parties and candidates? Theoretically, a 4% bump in support would be enough to tip close elections. Nonetheless, effectively isolating endorsements as a predictor of electoral success has eluded social scientists. To date, there is not overwhelming evidence that supports this notion that major celebrity endorsements guarantee electoral victories; otherwise, we would see a wave of Democratic candidates winning more elections. The benefits of celebrity endorsements are likely more indirect and context dependent.

One benefit of endorsements may have less to do with persuasion effects and more to do with civic engagement. In other words, endorsements have the power to increase voter registration and voter turnout. Researchers found that celebrity endorsements used in the 2004 U.S. presidential election increased the intent to vote among young Americans (Payne et al., 2007). Taylor Swift certainly had an impact on voter turnout during the 2018 midterm elections in Tennessee after backing congressional candidates in an Instagram post and encouraging people to vote during her acceptance speech at the American Music Awards. Swift's endorsements yielded an increase of 65,000 in registered voters in her home state (Harvey, 2018). Endorsements may not guarantee voters support the endorsed candidate but may nonetheless motivate an inattentive electorate to participate in politics (Wright, 2020).

Celebrity endorsements could especially help challengers close polling and enthusiasm gaps with frontrunners. For example, celebrity endorsements helped humanize the more rigid Al Gore in the 2000 election. Trailing frontrunner George W. Bush in January 2000 polls by a margin of 57 to 38%, Gore narrowed the gap six months later, polling at 44% relative to Bush's 48% (Gallup, 2000). During that time notable celebrity endorsements from Steven Spielberg, Harrison Ford, and Jack Nicholson helped renewed Gore momentum (Kettle, 2000). By election day, Gore would close the gap further, resulting in one of the closest elections in U.S. history. Gore would win the popular vote but lose the election. On a local level, Los Angeles mayoral candidate Rick Caruso narrowed the gap held by frontrunner Karen Bass in the 2022 election after a slew of endorsements from SoCal celebrities. Bass, a Democrat, won the closer-than-expected election with 54.8% of the votes.

Some researchers have attempted to quantify the impact a high-profile endorsement, like that of Oprah Winfrey's, could have on a campaign. Using magazine subscriptions and book sales as evidence of Oprah's reach, researchers found that her endorsement of Obama increased voter turnout, increased the number of financial contributions to the campaign, and helped the campaign earn one million additional votes for the Illinois Senator (Garthwaite & Moore, 2013). Pew (2007) noted that the Oprah effect may have been especially strong for voters leaning Democrat and for Black voters. And celebrity endorsements may be most persuasive for young or first-time voters (Wood & Herbst, 2007).

Making it difficult to discern the influence of celebrity endorsements is the validity of self-reported data and third-person effects. The **third-person effect** is the phenomenon in mass communication research that finds people tend to overstate the extent others are influenced by media while understating how they personally are affected by media content (Davison, 1983). For example, most Americans reported in 2007 that Oprah's endorsement would impact people's vote choice, yet 69% of those same survey participants reported that the endorsement would unlikely affect their personal vote (Pew, 2007). In other words, people believe they are somewhat immune to mediated persuasion, including appeals from celebrity endorsers. The bias of third-person effects was believed to drive self-reported responses in a study examining celebrity endorsements in the 2004 and 2008 U.S. presidential elections (Brubaker, 2011). Nonetheless, the electoral effects of celebrity endorsements are likely to be context dependent.

For an endorsement to yield persuasion effects, the celebrity must not only be highly familiar but also be perceived favorably by the public (Jackson, 2018). But the celebrities perceived as most familiar and favorable will vary according to demographic groups. In other words, whoever endorses you may be influential for one subgroup of voters but may not have universal credibility. For example, Pew (2007) found that 23% of voters under 30 would be more likely to support a candidate that was endorsed by *The Daily Show*'s Jon Stewart; Oprah held more credibility with Black voters; and celebrities are often perceived less favorably by Republican voters.

The decision to partner with celebrities should be determined by the subgroup of voters the campaign is attempting to engage. Campaigns are already beginning to make these considerations, seeking endorsers with clout in specific swing states or among specific subsects of voters. America Ferrera, for example, seen as especially favorable among women and Latino voters, endorsed the Biden-Harris campaign on Instagram, with a backdrop of campaign signs that read "Todos con Biden Harris." Trump sought support from Kid Rock in 2016 to help deliver the rocker's home state of Michigan. A Detroit native with a blue collar fanbase, Rock's endorsement in a critical swing state with a reliance on manufacturing would be perceived as more credible among Michigan voters than perhaps coastal celebrities.

Credibility aside, a celebrity endorsement will ensure that a candidate stays in the news cycle. Even if the endorsement is not persuading voters per se, generating news coverage is critical for lesser-known candidates and challengers. Endorsements in today's digital environment often go viral, generating mainstream news coverage and spectacle. This keeps candidates top of mind for low-information voters. Despite the welcome spectacle that stems from celebrity partnerships, these endorsements are not without risk for both the candidate and the endorser. That risk is heavier handed for Republican candidates.

Many conservative voters view celebrities as too "establishment" and representative of mainstream culture (Kornhaber, 2016). Both John McCain and Donald Trump often drew pejorative attention to the plethora of celebrity backers supporting their Democratic opponents. Popular culture is often caught in the crosshairs of a polarizing political climate and some celebrities can be symbolic of larger culture wars between the two parties: some garner widespread appeal from voters of one party but not the other. Entertainers, too, take risks by politically aligning with a candidate. Tom Brady, who kept a MAGA hat in his locker room during the 2016 U.S. presidential election ultimately walked back quotes he provided the media in support of a Trump presidency. He remained mum on Trump's 2020 reelection campaign, as the NFL quarterback was likely concerned about his legacy and social media backlash. Actress Susan Sarandon also faced online vitriol for her 2016 backing of Bernie Sanders (and later Jill Stein) over Democrat Hillary Clinton. Sarandon's endorsement came at a cost to her celebrity, rendering her a polarizing figure among women.

Despite mounting public pressure for celebrities to be more open and transparent about their politics, celebrities must calibrate the risk of alienating part of their fan base, and endorsing candidates may be especially risky business for entertainers who appear counter-culture or reliant on a particular region or demographic group for their commercial success (Coscarelli, 2016).

Summary

In today's entertainment-driven environment, campaigns are relying more heavily on partnerships with celebrities to court endorsements, access key segments of the electorate, remain in the news cycle, and drive people to the polls. In turn, there's also greater public pressure for celebrities to engage in politics thanks to social media and the direct access fans have to their idols. In doing so, celebrities often receive access or political influence. Whether motivated by ideology or access, celebrity plays a front-and-center role in the contemporary campaign. The result of an electorate drawn more to entertainment than news is the clamoring for more celebrity involvement in the campaign process.

We are seeing endorsements that are more visible and more creative, as celebrities adopt a more active approach to championing their candidate of choice. Celebrities are more than just check writers; they join the candidates on the campaign trail, they organize fundraising galas and headline rallies, they create viral content, and they act as surrogates of journalism by interviewing the candidates. In today's era of celebrity overload, even paid endorsements and courting online influencers are no longer off limits to campaigns. In a media environment where entertainment is the king, the role of celebrity will continue to be a force for how voters learn about candidates and how voters perceive them.

Resources and references

Abdullah, H. (2012, August 31). Eastwood, the empty chair and the speech everyone's talking about. *CNN*. www.cnn.com/2012/08/31/politics/eastwood-speech/index.html

Adams, W. [will.i.am]. (2008, February 2). *Yes we can Obama song by will.i.am* [Video]. YouTube. www.youtube.com/watch?v=2fZHou18Cdk

Aniftos, R. (2022, October 18). Beto O'Rourke hands Kasey Musgraves a beer during ACL festival. *Billboard*. www.billboard.com/music/music-news/beto-orourke-kasey-musgraves-beer-acl-festival-1235157690/

Behr, A. (2020, November 2). US election 2020: How the rival candidates have used music in their campaigns. *The Conversation*. https://theconversation.com/us-election-2020-how-the-rival-candidates-have-used-music-in-their-campaigns-149218

Biden, J. [Joe Biden]. (2020, October 16). *@JenniferLopez & Alex Rodriguez endorse Joe Biden for president 2020* [Video]. YouTube. www.youtube.com/watch?v=_28rjvdzEIE

Bradshaw, L. (2012, September 19). *Beyonce and Jay-Z host Barack Obama fundraiser at 40/40 club* [Video]. POPSUGAR Entertainment. www.youtube.com/watch?v=48mqwEPGnsI

Brooks, X. (2013, November 5). How Clint Eastwood's odd Obama speech turned Republican stomachs. *The Guardian*. www.theguardian.com/film/2013/nov/05/clint-eastwood-odd-obama-speech-republican-romney-convention

Brubaker, J. (2011). It doesn't affect my vote: Third-person effects of celebrity endorsements on college voters in the 2004 and 2008 presidential elections. *American Communication Journal, 13*(2), 4–22.

Cardi, B. [Bernie Sanders]. (2019, August 15). *Bernie x Cardi B* [Video]. YouTube. www. youtube.com/watch?v=p1ubTsrZFBU

Carroll, J. (2007, December 18). Clinton maintains large lead over Obama nationally. *Gallup.* https://news.gallup.com/poll/103351/clinton-maintains-large-lead-over-obama-nationally.aspx

Cioffi, C. (2022, August 3). To cameo or not to cameo? That's the question for political campaigns. *Roll Call.* https://rollcall.com/2022/08/03/to-cameo-or-not-question-for-political-campaigns/

Coscarelli, J. (2016, November 2). The campaign tour: Pop musicians get on the bus (mostly Clinton's). *The New York Times.* www.nytimes.com/2016/11/03/arts/music/election-concerts-jay-z-voter-registration.html

Cramer Brownell, K. (2014). *Showbiz politics: Hollywood in American political life.* UNC Press.

Davison, W. (1983). The third-person effect in communication. *Public Opinion Quarterly, 47*(1), 1–15.

Elberse, A., & Verleun, J. (2012). The economic value of celebrity endorsements. *Journal of Advertising Research, 52*(2), 149–165.

Gallup. (2000, June 22). The 2000 presidential election – a mid-year Gallup report. *Gallup.* https://news.gallup.com/poll/9898/2000-presidential-election-midyear-gallup-report.aspx

Garthwaite, C., & Moore, T. J. (2013). Can celebrity endorsements affect political outcomes? Evidence from the 2008 US democratic presidential primary. *Journal of Law, Economics, & Organization, 29*(2), 355–384.

Glaister, D., & Borger, J. (2004, April 2). Hollywood comes out for Kerry. *The Guardian.* www.theguardian.com/world/2004/apr/03/politics.uselections2004

Harvey, M. (2018). *Celebrity influence: Politics, persuasion, and issue-based advocacy.* University Press of Kansas.

Herndon, A. (2019, August 19). What do rally playlists say about the candidates? *The New York Times.* www.nytimes.com/interactive/2019/08/19/us/politics/presidential-campaign-songs-playlists.html

Jackson, D. J. (2018). The effects of celebrity endorsements of ideas and presidential candidates. *Journal of Political Marketing, 17*(4), 301–321.

Kettle, M. (2000, July 18). Hooray for Hollywood, says Gore, as stars Shun Bush. *The Guardian.* www.theguardian.com/world/2000/jul/19/filmnews.uselections2000

Kornhaber, S. (2016, November 13). Popular culture's failed presidential campaign. *The Atlantic.* www.theatlantic.com/entertainment/archive/2016/11/election-celebrities-trump-clinton-endorsements-beyonce-springsteen-david-jackson-bowling-green/507383/

Lee, M. J. (2012, August 30). Eastwood's rambling RNC speech. *Politico.* www.politico.com/story/2012/08/clint-eastwoods-rambling-gop-speech-080498

Noah, T. [The Daily Show]. (2022, June 6). *Votedemic 2022: L.A.'s mayoral race* [Video]. YouTube. www.youtube.com/watch?app=desktop&v=sIFO0a0nVb4&t=0h6m58s

Payne, J. G., Hanlon, J. P., & Twomey, D. P. (2007). Celebrity spectacle influence on young voters in the 2004 presidential campaign: What to expect in 2008. *American Behavioral Scientist, 50*(9), 1239–1246.

Pew. (2007, September 20). *The Oprah factor and campaign 2008. Do political endorsements matter?* Pew Research Center. www.pewresearch.org/politics/2007/09/20/the-oprah-factor-and-campaign-2008/

Staggs, B. (2020, February 6). Politicians are using cameo to pay celebrities to make video endorsements, and it's all legal. *The Orange County Register.* www.ocregister.com/2020/02/06/did-that-celebrity-really-endorse-that-candidate-the-video-cant-be-trusted/

Wallsten, K. (2010). "Yes we can": How online viewership, blog discussions, campaign statements, and mainstream media coverage produced a viral video phenomenon. *Journal of Information Technology & Politics, 7*(2–3), 163–181.

Wood, N. T., & Herbst, K. C. (2007). Political star power and political parties: Does celebrity endorsement win first-time votes? *Journal of Political Marketing, 6*(2–3), 141–158.

Wright, L. (2020). *Star power: American democracy in the age of the celebrity candidate.* Routledge.

6 The instaworthy campaign

Gaming, streaming, and social media

Long ago in a social media galaxy far, far away, MySpace was top dog, Facebook was limited to college kids with an Ivy League email address, and Reddit, Snapchat, Instagram, Twitter, YouTube, and TikTok would be months or years away from launching. Another social media relic also inhabited the digital space a couple decades ago: Meetup.com. Meetup operated as an online forum where like-minded folks with similar hobbies and interests could build community and organize offline interactions. Meetups were created for book clubs, board game groups, rock climbing, and even political campaigns. The website is largely responsible for catapulting a physician and former governor from liberal Vermont to the forefront of the 2004 Democratic primaries.

Howard Dean had little to no name recognition on the national stage and his politics were considered left of the party, but one campaign advantage he had over his opponents was that he harnessed the power of digital tools. His campaign developed Meetup groups to engage in digital advocacy for the candidate and foster community through blogs, volunteer-led events, debate watch parties, and other offline actions. The campaign's ability to generate momentum was attributed to the transfer of online social interactions to offline activities, or "electronic-to-face" interactions (Weinberg & Williams, 2006). The second critical component of the digital media strategy was aimed at decentralizing the campaign structure to empower supporters and volunteers.

According to *Wired* (2004), Dean's campaign manager Joe Trippi leveraged Meetup to diffuse the hierarchy within campaign operations. That decentralized approach entrusted volunteers to do much of the heavy lifting. Trippi held monthly conference calls with supporters organizing events and provided campaign materials, but the volunteers ultimately took the lead. Supporters wrote letters to neighbors and friends and used Meetup to build an online network that would be used for organizing offline campaign events. From February 2003 to fall 2003, the number of offline campaign meetups increased from 11 to 800 – all organized and coordinated by supporters rather than paid staffers (Wired, 2004). The digital strategy bolstered Dean's authenticity, and its grassroots appeal helped the candidate secure labor union endorsements and facilitate a high volume of small financial donations. By the end of August 2003, Dean

DOI: 10.4324/9781003364832-6

had passed Democratic frontrunners Dick Gephardt and John Kerry in early primary polling.

If Dean's digital campaign was so groundbreaking, then why haven't you heard of him? Well, digital media provide campaign affordances and limitations. After falling short in the Iowa caucus, an overzealous Dean delivered an aggressive speech to maintain optimism among his supporters. With shouting, a strained voice, and an unusual howl that is often referred to as the "Dean scream," the howling candidate went viral for all the wrong reasons. The nonstop footage shared online and on cable news was suggestive of the candidate being radical or even a little unhinged. In short, digital media helped the Dean momentum spread like wildfire but his campaign for the Democratic nomination was snuffed out quickly by that same technology. Although Dean hit a ceiling before reaching the general election, his campaign revealed innovative strategies for helping a relatively unknown candidate build momentum through modest means – small donations and a diffused network of supporters that moved online support to offline activities. In many ways, the Dean campaign's use of Meetup.com foreshadowed Barack Obama's 2008 campaign website.

Social media savvy: YouTube, Twitter, and beyond

Four years after Dean's groundbreaking campaign, the tension between legacy news outlets and online information sources reached a tipping point. Pew data show that, by 2008, nearly 60% of voters were seeking political information through various digital tools including email, social media, and instant messaging (Smith, 2009). Meanwhile, traditional news outlets were losing some of its influence as a trusted source of political information and politically engaged news consumers were seeking ideologically confirming sources of news online – a phenomenon known as **selective exposure**. For better or worse, the importance of digital and social media in electoral politics exploded after the 2004 U.S. presidential election, with Obama often dubbed the Facebook president. By the 2020 presidential election, digital tools and spaces were even more paramount as campaigns navigated limitations during the COVID-19 pandemic. No longer could candidates rely on a strong **ground game**, or face-to-face canvassing, as digital spaces largely replaced offline campaigning during the pandemic. Although social media following and influence cannot always predict electoral success, social media savvy affords campaigns a crucial advantage.

One of the first indicators that Obama was fully embracing the digital space was the hiring of Chris Hughes, a 24-year-old co-founder of Facebook, to help design his campaign website. MyBarackObama.com would function like a social-networking site and included tools for users to download lists of potential supporters within their zip codes, report conversations users had with potential supporters, and create blogs, groups, and post images. The campaign site squarely focused on community and interactivity, mirroring Dean's approach by empowering volunteers. Like Dean's Meetup.com structure, Obama's platform helped supporters to connect and organize. MyBarackObama.com served as a source for campaign video content, podcasts, and interactive forums. By the end of the 2008 campaign, MyBarackObama helped approximately 35,000 different groups across the country organize more than 200,000 events on his behalf (Havenstein, 2008).

And Obama went all in on social media. In addition to Facebook, his campaign leveraged MySpace, Twitter, Flickr, Digg, BlackPlanet, LinkedIn, AsianAve, MiGente, and Glee, reflecting a social media war chest inclusive of mass platforms with broad appeal and more narrowly targeted niche platforms (Dutta & Fraser, 2008). The campaign churned out more than 1,820 YouTube videos during the 2008 campaign, and the social media content produced by the Obama campaign far outpaced Hillary Clinton's campaign and the campaigns of Republican frontrunners John McCain and Mitt Romney (Gulati, 2009). Moreover, the power of social media would not be lost on President Obama's administration and his 2012 reelection campaign.

During his presidency, the White House functioned as a digital media force, operating official social media accounts for Obama and his cabinet, public facing heads of federal agencies, and even staffers at the U.S. State Department. Social media became the primary tool for speaking directly to the public, communicating policy, and engaging in diplomacy. For example, the administration teased the president's 2015 State of the Union address by posting 18 online videos and supplementing the speech with dozens of online slides (Eilperin, 2015). And when it was time to communicate Obama's paid family leave policy, the administration bypassed mainstream news to release the information and instead turned to LinkedIn because of the high number of working women using the platform.

Obama's 2012 campaign expanded its social media toolset. A greater emphasis was placed on Instagram during the reelection campaign. *The New York Times* reported that Obama attracted 1.4 million Instagram followers relative to his Republican opponent, Massachusetts Governor Mitt Romney's 38,000 followers (Wortham, 2012). The campaign also innovated by developing a Reddit presence to reach young voters. The community-driven forum became the venue for Obama to participate in an "Ask Me Anything" event that fielded questions from Reddit users ranging from student loan debt to federal assistance for small businesses. The forum, upvoted by more than 200,000 Reddit users, also blended the personal: Obama answered questions about beer and basketball. His campaign also hosted a 2011 Twitter town hall event moderated by platform cofounder Jack Dorsey. There, Obama addressed questions focused on the economy, jobs, the federal deficit, and government spending from accounts using the event's #AskObama hashtag. According to Pew (2013), the Obama campaign published 25 times as many posts to Twitter than the Romney campaign, providing the president a tool to shape campaign narratives without relying much on mainstream news. The reelection campaign's strategic use of social media platforms was novel for presidential politics, but Obama's campaign simply reflected the media habits of the electorate.

Pew noted a jump in registered voters following candidates and politicians from 6% in 2010 to 16% in 2014, with an even higher percentage for voters under 30 (Anderson, 2015). In other words, a greater slice of the electorate was bypassing traditional news media to connect with candidates and political figures. Additionally, the percentage of voters using mobile devices to access campaign information increased from 13% in 2010 to 28% in 2014 and, again, with an even higher percentage of users in young demographic groups (Smith, 2014). As news consumption continued to migrate toward mobile and digital platforms, social media was becoming ripe for strategic political campaign communication. By the 2016 presidential election, campaigns were tinkering with several social media platforms to engage voters reach the politically inattentive, and convey authenticity.

For example, Clinton's 2016 campaign was active on Pinterest, sharing family photos, honoring pioneering women, and posting snapshots from the campaign trail. The social networking site, especially popular among women, helped the campaign soften the candidate's image while attracting thousands of followers. Both Republican Jeb Bush and Clinton were among the first candidates to use Snapchat to formally announce their presidential campaigns. Both utilized the Snapchat live story feature which activates video content for 24 hours; Republicans John Kasich and Scott Walker, Rand Paul, and Marco Rubio also tinkered with the Snapchat platform. But no social media tool would be more influential during the 2016 election than Twitter. Donald Trump's prolific Twitter use helped him dominate the news cycle, control narratives, and establish authenticity with disengaged voters (see **Case Study 6.1**). In fact, political analysts and the former president have acknowledged that he would not be president without the microblogging platform.

Case Study 6.1   Trump tweets his way to the White House

In the first debate of the Republican primaries, Donald Trump was asked why he had donated to prominent Democrats prior to running for president as a Republican. The response Trump offered was "our system is broken." He went on to explain that he donated to candidates of both parties in exchange for influence and access. In other words, he bought them off. This critique of Washington would embody the rhetoric of Trump's 2016 campaign, which often chimed "drain the swamp." The narrative of Trump as Washington outsider became paramount to his campaign and Trump loudly voiced his contempt for lifelong politicians and democratic institutions – including the press. But with social media emerging as platforms with even greater reach than news outlets, the Trump campaign didn't need to cooperate with mainstream

Figure 6.1 Donald Trump posts thousands of tweets to Twitter, sidestepping traditional news media to control campaign narratives.

Source: Illustration by Eduardo Rangel.

media. On Twitter, Trump already had a captive audience developed through his foray into reality television: NBC's *The Apprentice*. On Twitter, Trump bypassed mainstream news and molded his own narratives. He could double-down on outlandish claims or vitriolic attacks. He wasn't accountable to journalists or even his campaign strategists. He would tweet at odd hours of the day, sometimes in jumbled grammatical structure, misspellings, and factual inaccuracies. He would loft public attacks on journalists, public officials, and elite celebrities to further reinforce his outsider narrative. His unchecked use of Twitter suggested to voters a certain level of authenticity. And as a prominent celebrity, almost any tactical move or comment he made on social media became instant headlines in the news cycle, meaning his prolific tweets benefited from amplification effects from mainstream news, essentially guaranteeing extensive press coverage while still allowing the candidate to maintain distance from democratic institutions. This strategy gave voters the perception of a grassroots, populist outsider. Even those who vehemently disagreed with Trump's tone, rhetoric, or vision for America would share tweets widely, creating a second wind of amplification through **outrage sharing**. In 2016, Trump was the second most used keyword in tweets made by Democratic members of Congress and was the top term during the 2020 campaign; meanwhile, Clinton and Biden did not crack the top ten keywords used by Republican members of Congress (Pew, 2021). He continued with the preferred communication method of tweeting once in office, posting to the platform 5,300 times between June 2016 and November 2017 (Collins, 2018)

Both the 2016 and 2020 U.S. presidential elections were record breaking years for funds spent on social media advertising. In 2016, Clinton and Trump spent a combined $81 million on ads across social media platforms, and those figures ballooned in 2020, with Trump spending $107 million and Biden $94 million (Manthey, 2020). Prioritizing social media over mainstream news engagement is now the new norm. This is evident from how candidates are sharing the news of their campaigns. In June 2023, scholar/activist Cornell West announced his presidential campaign through Twitter. In February 2023, Republican candidate Nikki Haley, former U.S. ambassador to the United Nations and former South Carolina governor, announced her bid for the White House in a video posted to Twitter and YouTube. Even sitting President Joe Biden overlooked traditional news outlets to formally share his reelection campaign, making his official announcement in a video posted to Twitter and YouTube in April 2023. The direct announcement allowed Biden to control the narratives and steer the conversation toward values and culture issues such as recent threats to reproductive rights and conservative led book bans. The latest iteration of social media has some candidates tinkering with TikTok's campaign capabilities.

In 2022, 40% of gubernatorial candidates had a TikTok account; 47% of Democratic congressional candidates had an account and 12% of Republican congressional candidates (Gorman & Miller, 2022). In a race Democrats were hopeful of flipping, Georgia gubernatorial candidate Stacey Abrams was active on the platform. TikTok was also a battleground for the tightly contested Pennsylvania U.S. Senate race, with John Fetterman (D) and Mehmet Oz (R) using TikTok videos as a low-cost platform for attack ads. TikTok's political influence is expected to grow in 2024. In fact, one challenger to Biden has already embraced the trendy platform. Author and presidential candidate Marianne Williamson has posted 65 TikTok videos and has attracted 11 million viewers to her account as of April 2023 (Grim, 2023). Now, the longshot Democratic challenger is polling above 20% with voters under the age of 30 – a sizable increase from her 2020 campaign (Grim, 2023). Although Williamson is unlikely to win the nomination, her campaign understands the TikTok audience, focusing on issues that matter most to young voters including student loan debt and federal marijuana policy. At the very least, her social media strategy could influence the issue priorities of the Democratic frontrunner.

Understanding both the platform and the audience is critical for engaging with voters through social media. TikTok videos should appear less polished and less scripted and should reflect the zeitgeist of the medium, meaning that videos could seem amateurish or awkward. The TikTok audience skews young, and campaigns need to have their pulse on the audience for platforms they leverage. That's why Ohio U.S. Senate candidate Tim Ryan turned to his teenage daughter to get started on the app (Kambhampaty, 2022). Ryan, a low-key and folksy Democrat, would soon post videos featuring snippets of his speeches to the tune of Taylor Swift songs. Knowing the tastes of your audience also explains why communications staff for Massachusetts Senator Ed Markey pushed a TikTok plea for support of the Green New Deal to the electronic vibes of Odesza. These social media tactics even trickle down to lower-level elections. Just ask the young campaign staffers responsible for operating the social media accounts for Los Angeles Controller Kenneth Mejia.

Mejia, a 32-year-old political unknown, prioritized social media to educate young voters about his candidacy and the functions of a city controller. Twitter, Instagram, and TikTok were among the platforms used to implement the campaign's unconventional strategy. Posts included the candidate dressed in Pikachu costumes, dancing to BTS songs, dogs, and lots of gym selfies (Park & Smith, 2022). Mejia, with a following of 18,000 Instagram users, routinely shared flexing bicep posts and video footage of the candidate pumping iron. The stars of Mejia's campaign were his two corgis – one which even appeared in his swearing in video. Opponents scoffed at how personally revealing his campaign accounts were. Unabashed in his strategy, Mejia doubled down on his hyper-personalized campaign by creating a TikTok with the text "when they don't think you're a candidate because you wear a tank top [fire image]" set to the tune of a Harry Styles "Watermelon Sugar" cover. Mejia's 2022 city controller campaign catapulted him to public office over well-known city councilor Paul Koretz by adapting to the social spaces and eliminating buffers between the private and public persona of the candidate.

One critical lesson these campaigns teach us is the importance of not waiting for disengaged voters to meet you at *your* digital spaces but, rather, to go inhabit *theirs*. We see evidence in this as campaigns migrate from Facebook to Instagram, Snapchat, TikTok, and even niche digital platforms that reach disengaged voters. Incorporating meme and influencer strategies offers yet another pathway of meeting these groups in their own digital spaces.

All eyes on me: selfies, memes, and influencers

GloZell Green rose to internet stardom after publishing content on YouTube as early as 2008, long before "influencer" was a household word. Known for her signature green lipstick, she built a rapport with her audience by sharing thoughts on web trends, performing comedic impersonations and exuding an unpretentious style that especially resonated with Millennials. Sick-leave policy and economic recovery were never exactly the bread and butter of her YouTube channel but were the talking points of a January 2015 interview with President Obama. Cybersecurity, police brutality, immigration, and same-sex marriage were also balanced in the conversation with lighthearted comedic moments, with Green clumsily referring to Michelle Obama as the president's "first wife" rather than "first lady." Such candid moments of laughter humanized the president, while allowing Obama to narrate his legacy, highlight administrative achievements and establish good will between the public and Democratic Party in advance of the 2016 U.S. presidential election.

Why prioritize White House access for influencers like Green over journalists? Green has a following of more than 4 million – at least four or five times that of what a typical White House correspondent might have. And a sit down with an influencer is far more likely to go viral and circulate digitally among low information voters.

Spending time with influencers bolsters a politician's perceived authenticity and allows them to exploit the built-in network of these online celebrities. That audience is so coveted that campaigns are crafting influencer strategies. For example, Joe Biden's 2020 campaign hired the firm Village Marketing to develop an influencer strategy to improve turnout among young voters. Tapping into influencer networks helped the Biden campaign extend its communications reach despite having fewer followers on its official social media accounts than Trump. The campaign included brief segments and recorded conversations between Biden and lifestyle, fashion, and pop culture influencers with more than millions of followers but also between Biden and **nano influencers** with a more narrowly defined community of followers in the thousands. For campaigns, they aren't necessarily banking on a direct or explicit endorsement but, rather, access to a network of trusting followers. For example, Biden's collaboration with influencer Beth Mota granted the campaign reach of more than 4 million followers.

The social reach of online influencers is increasingly useful to political campaigns as Americans continue to confine much of their media diets to digital and social spaces. Content from influencers isn't the only way to increase candidate visibility and create eye-catching moments. Campaigns have looked to other byproducts of influencer culture: selfies and memes (**see Case Study 6.2**).

Case Study 6.2 Elizabeth Warren strategizes "selfies"

Figure 6.2 Elizabeth Warren connects with voters by posing for thousands of selfies along the campaign trail, with supporters sharing to social media.

Source: Illustration by Eduardo Rangel.

The traditional way of thinking about photo ops on the campaign trail conjures the image of candidates shaking hands and kissing babies. For Massachusetts U.S. Senator Elizabeth Warren, it meant standing for upwards of 4 hours after events to pose with supporters in a self-described "selfie line." Whereas some candidates offer only a select few handshakes or require a financial contribution for a photo, Warren's 2020 presidential campaign insisted on providing equitable access to hundreds lingering after events. The personalization of these meets and greets neatly fit her campaign's populist and inclusive narratives. The Warren selfie lines became a mainstay of her campaign events, involving eight staffers to organize the line, collect people's bags and phones, snapping the shot, and returning their belongings (Jennings, 2019). The campaign reported that Warren reached 100,000 "selfies" by January 2020. The selfie strategy aligned with her populist vision, humanized the candidate, personalized the election for supporters, and made Warren incredibly approachable. And it increased buy in for volunteers by providing them with a tangible memory of their labor. The selfie keepsakes came with more longevity than a simple handshake, a fleeting moment that can't necessarily be shared on social media. But those thousands of selfies enjoyed a longer shelf life as they were shared by supporters across social media platforms and on official campaign accounts. Warren was provided with a moment to build rapport with voters and those in line were provided rare access to a presidential candidate. The novelty of the "selfie line" approach also generated a plethora of positively toned news stories. *The New York Times* even ran a "how to" about the novel approach titled "How to get a selfie with Elizabeth Warren in 8 steps." Once Warren reached the 100,000-selfie milestone, social media and mainstream news were buzzing with coverage.

Stepping up one's meme game also plays a part in contemporary campaign strategy. In February 2020, Michael Bloomberg's presidential campaign hired online marketing companies Tribe, a platform that pays influencers to sponsor content, and Meme 2020, a digital marketing venture led by Mick Purzycki, the chief executive of the company responsible for the infamous Fyre Festival viral marketing campaign. Strategically curated interactions with administrators of popular meme accounts generated a series of campaign memes aimed at making the 77-year-old candidate appear more relatable to young voters while tapping the massive following of these users. The campaign included meme engagements with DoYouEvenLift, MiddleClassFancy, ShitheadSteve, White-PeopleHumor, GrapeJuiceBoys, and FuckJerry (Lorenz, 2020). By momentarily hijacking these audiences, the Bloomberg campaign generated content with a reach of 4.6 million (WhitePeopleHumor), 7 million (ShitheadSteve), and 17 million followers (FuckJerry).

The meme campaign is one example of leveraging social and digital media as a means for showing authenticity and relatability. They afford candidates low-cost platforms for shaping political narratives and speaking to the voters directly without the filters and editing of mainstream news media. And other digital platforms can put the candidate directly in the driver's seat of the dialogue.

Being seen *and* heard: podcasts and digital shorts

Ahead of his 2020 presidential campaign, Cory Booker hosted his own podcast through Audacy, a free online radio-streaming platform. The "Lift Every Voice" podcast was published from January 2018 through February 2019 – up until the official launch of his campaign. Invited guests included celebrities, activists, community organizers, and influential political elites. Booker's first episode featured a conversation with the late U.S. Representative John Lewis. The podcast functioned as a pre-campaign campaign, allowing Booker to create discourse surrounding his values and issue priorities. Episodes centered on social justice and equality – themes that would ultimately align with his campaign message of unity. And candidates and politicians from both sides of the aisle have begun to realize that the power podcasts have to help craft narratives and influence public discourse.

Republican members of Congress Dan Crenshaw and Matt Gaetz host their own podcasts, "Hold These Truths" and "Firebrand." Texas Senator and former presidential candidate Ted Cruz cohosts a podcast that taps into his brand of outrage conservatism. Democratic Representation Jim Clyburn streams his "Clyburn Chronicles" and 2020 presidential candidates Marianne Williamson, Julian Castro, and Andrew Yang all dabbled in podcasting. For two full years, Vermont Senator Bernie Sanders turned to podcasting to remain part of the national discourse between his two presidential campaigns in 2016 and 2020. Hillary Clinton and Pete Buttigieg looked to iHeartRadio for their podcasts, "You and Me Both with Hillary Clinton" and "The Defining Decade."

As politicians have only recently incorporated podcasts in the last few election cycles, audiences for these programs remain small, and political strategists are struggling to strike the right tone (Quah, 2020; Robertson, 2022). The most successful podcasts are fluid, conversational, and nimble – characteristics that counter the tightly controlled nature of campaigns. The blending of politics and personality is an imperative of a successful political podcast; however, most politicians take an overly cautious approach and use podcasting as strategic extensions of a memoir (Quah, 2020). That approach may help craft political narratives about their roots, family, and vision but is unlikely to entertain audiences for the length of a typical podcast. While most candidates don't necessarily have the personality or media know-how to host a home-run podcast, they can always appear as guests to tap into larger audiences without the pressures of hosting.

Booker, for example, not only hosted his own podcast but also prioritized appearances across a number of others. Booker appeared as a guest on the NPR Politics podcast, The Political Party Live podcast (based in Iowa) – shortly after announcing his candidacy in 2019 – and the Yes, Girl podcast. These programs helped Booker steer campaign narratives on issues like gun control and social justice. Outgoing president Barack Obama was a surprise guest on episode 613 on the "WTF" podcast with comedian Marc Maron. No longer campaigning for his own electoral outcomes, the appearance helped Obama to bolster the brand of the Democratic Party in advance of the 2016 election and cement the legacy of his two-term presidency. Obama's conversation touched not only on racism, gun violence, and congressional gridlock but also on light-hearted topics. The novelty of the guest appearance generated national news and online buzz for both the president and for Maron. Perhaps no candidate has relished the chatter of podcasting more than conspiracy theorist prone Robert F. Kennedy, Jr., whose appearance on *The Joe Rogan Experience* catapulted him into the national conversation as he challenges Biden in the 2024 Democratic primaries.

Obama's digital-media strategy astutely gave equal footing to both light-hearted, humanizing uses as well as policy discourse. In 2015, Obama collaborated with Buzzfeed to produce "Things everybody does but doesn't talk about." The video features relatable moments including the president practicing his pronunciation of February and using a selfie stick. Creating the digital short required 10 minutes from the president for filming yet generated more than 22 million views within the first 24 hours of publishing (Jarvey, 2015). Buzzfeed ran the video across its social media accounts and published it in listicle story format with the following disclaimer: "How did we get Obama to use a selfie stick? Oh, because he wants you to go to https:///www.healthcare.gov. The success of that video led to a second digital short with Buzzfeed in 2016 aimed at encouraging young people to vote. The video features Obama participating in "5 activities harder to do than registering to vote," and begins with the president struggling to play the anxiety-inducing board game "Operation." But Obama was not the first politician to recognize the potential of digital shorts.

A bipartisan collaboration between New Jersey Republican Governor Chris Christie and Democratic Senator Cory Booker resulted in a 2012 digital short, long ahead of both politician's presidential campaigns. The video centers on Christie's staff strategizing for a comeback in the polls. Every stunt the team concocts, Booker beats them to the punch. When Christie's car gets a flat tire,

Booker is already by his side fixing it. When a baby falls from a balcony, Booker is there to catch it. The digital short taps into the "frenemies" dynamic between the two New Jersey politicians, with Christie scowling and staring into the camera, stating "Booker" with disdain and frustration. The video somewhat parodies the campaign process, in turn making both politicians seem relatable and ordinary. The video published to the "GovChristie" YouTube account, attracting nearly a half a million views. Both Christie and Booker would go on to win reelection in 2014, but fall short in their bids for the White House in 2016 and 2020. Booker most recently teamed with Democratic Senator Jon Tester in similarly toned digital shorts drawing attention to their legislation looking to reign in agriculture consolidation and, more importantly, increase enthusiasm for Tester's 2024 reelection campaign in Montana.

President Joe Biden partnered with HBO and Julia Luis-Dreyfuss, the actress portraying fictional vice president Selena Meyer on the show *Veep*, to create a comical take on the feeling of being vice president while aspiring to be president. The digital short featured a bevy of beltway cameos and although the video was produced for the 2014 White House Correspondents Dinner with the Washington press corps, the production value and the strategic cameos suggest a larger audience in mind. The video went viral, shared by news and entertainment media in addition to official White House social media accounts and C-SPAN. When HBO shared the clip as part of a promo for *Veep*, more than 3 million viewed the video on YouTube.

Digital shorts should only play a more prominent role in upcoming elections with TikTok emerging as a dominant platform for video. Also emerging as a relatively untapped campaign tool is the gaming industry, as candidates are just beginning to allocate advertising resources to video games and use their fandom for gaming franchises to fuel connections with young voters.

Gaming the (political) system

Obama's 2008 campaign was not only innovative with its social media engagement but also leaned into gaming culture. The campaign was the first to purchase ads in video games. As gaming transitioned from console to digital play, candidates could leverage the industry in ways that would help them target groups not easily identified by political campaigns.

With a desire to engage with young men in the 18–34 demographic, the Obama campaign used Xbox Live to target this group in ten states with early voting (Gorman, 2008). The Obama ads – embedded as banner ads or billboards – were strategically placed in games popular with young men, including *NASCAR 09*, *Guitar Hero 3*, *NFL Tour*, and *NBA Live 08*. For example, an Obama ad in *NBA Live* appeared as a banner donning the front of the statisticians' courtside table with his image and a web address: voteforchange.org. The COVID-19 pandemic that first ravaged the world in 2020 accelerated the already-increasing appeal of gaming as a mass communication industry. Stay-at-home orders helped broaden demographics of users and games became therapeutic escapes during a time of uncertainty and social isolation. Seizing on the burgeoning industry, the Biden-Harris campaign released virtual campaign yard signs in September 2020. Through the Nintendo Switch app, users could access one of four uniquely designed virtual signs that they could adorn their virtual homes with within the *Animal Crossing: New Horizons* game – one of several games that swiftly gained popularity during the pandemic.

While embedded game ads remain largely untapped, they could bring even greater customization to campaign advertising strategy. Games are also a way for campaigns to reach a more apolitical audience, coaxing new supporters and first-time voters to the electoral process. Although gaming communities tend to maintain politically neutral digital spaces, some politicians see gaming live streams as a creative platform to connect with young voters and tap the followers of elite gamers.

One popular stay-at-home-order pastime, *Among Us*, became a surprise social gaming hit during the pandemic with the objective being for a team of players to identify and kill the designated mole. Junior congresswoman Alexandria Ocasio-Cortez assembled her own *Among Us* "squad" with colleague Ilhan Omar, a U.S. representative from Minnesota and Anys (a Twitch player with more than 6 million followers). Other high-profile users teaming up with AOC included DrLupo and Pokimane – both with multi-million person followings on Twitch (Frank, 2020). By using the live-streaming platform, Ocasio-Cortez engaged with a relatively apolitical community not typically addressed by politicians. Her monologue as she navigated the game reminded fans of their experience learning the game and demonstrated her authenticity among a young core of potential voters. Viewers could engage with Ocasio-Cortez by participating in a lively chat feed and although she mostly steered away from politics during the live stream, AOC casually plugged healthcare reform and the Biden-Harris ticket. By infiltrating *their* digital spaces, the live Twitch stream attracted more than 400,000 viewers for Ocasio-Cortez (D'Anastasio, 2020) and the amplification effects of live streams can offer a much bigger reach. The GameSpot YouTube channel posted a montage of the best AOC Twitch moments, providing their 5.2 million followers with exposure to the congresswoman; the gaming community responded with 31,000 likes.

A member of the U.S. House of Representatives even credits gaming with helping him win a tight 2018 election. California Democrat Josh Harder is considered the top gamer in Congress, with a presence on *League of Legends, Crusader Kings*, and *Football Manager* (Smith, 2020). Harder's use of Twitch and Snapchat ads embody the creative avenues that candidates are using to engage young voters digitally. With the U.S. House skewing younger than the Senate, gaming is playing a more public role in how junior members of congress connect with voters. Former U.S. Representative Jared Polis, now governor of Colorado, embraces his fandom for the *League of Legends* and participates in the multiplayer game with constituents, users overseas, and even former colleagues in Congress. California reps Democrat Scott Peters and Republican Darrell Issa even dueled it out with *Mario Kart* at the 2017 Comic-Con in San Diego (Nelson, 2018). The friendly competition led to news attention and demonstrated a symbolic gesture of camaraderie and bipartisanship in an especially polarized political climate.

From the gaming industry to influencers, and widespread campaign adoption of social media, political communication's tango with these diverse digital tools begs the following question: What are the effects of these ever-evolving digital strategies? What does it mean for campaigns and for voters?

Assessing the campaign effectiveness of social and digital media tools

Without having much history to draw from, campaigns do not have the clearest of pictures in terms of which digital tools are most effective. Furthermore, platform preferences of the electorate remain in constant flux. Facebook was paramount to Obama's 2008 victory, yet it was Twitter holding more influence by 2016. And by 2024, the number of users of these early social platforms has plateaued, as these technological diversions take a back seat to emerging tools like TikTok and even ChatGPT, an artificial intelligence tool quickly capturing the attention of the electorate. In many ways, digital political campaign communication remains in a trial-and-error phase. How effective these tools are in influencing electoral outcomes is unclear, despite some anecdotal successes.

Certainly, Howard Dean found short-term success through Meetup.com. For those who attended campaign Meetup events for Dean, the result was an increase in volunteerism, campaign donations, and advocacy both on and offline (Weinberg & Williams, 2006). Those tools fell short of electing Dean but were effective in introducing him to the national stage and helping him become the temporary Democratic frontrunner. Obama would fare better in 2008, with the campaign's investment in Facebook. McCain spent more time engaging with traditional media, trailing behind Obama's social media followers by a 4-to-1 margin. Exit polls indicated that 70% of voters under the age of 25 voted for Obama – the highest percentage since the inception of exit polls in 1976 (Dutta & Fraser, 2008). These examples reinforce research indicating that digital tools help reduce barriers for challengers, raise funds, and help close the advantage that incumbents and better-known candidates have (Petrova et al., 2021). Digital media helped Obama defeat more established candidates in 2008, including Hillary Clinton and John McCain, and helped Dean surpass more prominent candidates in the early stages of the 2004 primaries. Indirectly, social and digital media can make elections more competitive, but that doesn't necessarily mean that voters are always learning about candidates or being persuaded by their online campaign content.

For example, an experimental study found no significant difference in levels of political knowledge between Facebook users exposed to political news relative to those who were not (Feezell & Ortiz, 2021). Other researchers suggest learning about campaigns through social media could be platform dependent. For example, some knowledge gains were observed for Twitter users while declines were found for Facebook users (Boukes, 2019). In other words, some affordances of social media could be overstated. Further complicating the debate of digital campaign effectiveness, not all social media companies are transparent with analytics data. Snapchat and Tumblr, for example, don't share the number of followers a user has, and given that Snapchat posts are temporary, and they are less likely to be captured or go viral rendering it difficult to fully measure their reach. Fleeting communication and temporary stories are difficult to measure, but perhaps the more important function of digital media is for candidates to simply have a presence on them to convey relatability and show they understand the world and media environment their constituents live in.

A fun and interactive social media account may not persuade people to change their vote, but digital tools can mobilize a candidate's base and those already receptive to their agenda (Eilperin, 2015). When it comes to campaign strategy, narrowly tailoring communication is the name of the game for social media. If a campaign is looking to reach groups inactive in electoral politics, the campaigns must take their messages to the digital spaces these groups inhabit. Simply being savvy enough to inhabit these spaces and use them competently may indicate to voters that a candidate has a better understanding of *their* world, and the issues that their community feels are important. Digital platforms also function as critical tools for humanizing politicians, regardless of how establishment they seem. Hillary Clinton's social media profiles, for example, routinely describe her as a "grandmother," "hair icon," and "pantsuit afficionado" above politician. By simply joining Twitter in 2013, Clinton made national news headlines for mainstream outlets including *ABC*, *Time*, and *The Washington Post*. The humanizing effect may shine best when candidates put politics on the back burner and prioritize the personal. Apps and social media that use temporary story functions may be especially effective at humanizing a candidate, because their fleeting nature limits the advertising component of the post.

Use of social-media platforms also comes with the added benefit of data collection. Even if candidates' strategic use of digital media isn't directly leading to new supporters or votes, the data collected from these platforms can inform more traditional elements of political campaign communication and help campaigns better activate existing supporters. The data collection boon can also come from in-house apps.

The Trump campaign app launched in 2016 and through the 2020 election surpassed 1 million downloads (Brigham, 2020). Biden also unveiled an app of his own in 2020. Both of their apps collect users' names, emails, and their geographic locations. The campaigns can filter data according to vote history and party affiliation. Some campaigns are even tapping Beacontrac, a company that installs Bluetooth beacons in lawn signs or at events to collect information from the smartphones of people passing by (Brigham, 2020). The tool, for example, has been used to identify churchgoers unregistered to vote. Such digital tools can collect data that helps politicians narrowly target their campaign communication and guide where to allocate precious campaign resources. As data become a prolific part of the campaign equation, candidates must be cautious about third party companies their campaigns tap. That's one lesson learned from the Cambridge Analytica scandal.

During the 2016 presidential election, most Facebook users were unaware of U.K.-based company Cambridge Analytica, a data-driven political consultancy firm. But the company would quickly become a household name and subject of congressional hearings on data privacy. The firm specialized in using psychographics to help campaigns target messages. **Psychographics** went beyond the norms of microtargeting with demographic information by culling copious data to generate personality and lifestyle profiles of users. The company pulled information from approximately 50 million Facebook users while violating the tech company's terms of service to discreetly collect information of friends of friends who were taking personality quizzes. After *The Guardian* broke the story that the Ted Cruz campaign used Cambridge Analytica data collected through nefariously means, national news outlets joined in a chorus of investigative stories (see Davies, 2015). That reporting ultimately generated negative publicity not only for Cruz but also for Facebook and Trump's campaign, which had also tapped Cambridge Analytica for data. Both campaigns had to distance themselves from the company.

Certainly, use of any digital media is not free of campaign risks. It isn't uncommon for candidates – particularly those who skew older or are less experienced with emerging technologies – to have digital missteps or struggle with the spontaneity of these social technologies. And public response on social media feedback loops can be unforgiving.

When former Florida governor Jeb Bush ran for president in 2016, he was often seen as the more cerebral and nerdier brother to George W. Bush. In an election cycle where candidates from all political spectrums were flocking to digital and social media, his campaign saw YouTube as a platform for humanizing him with young voters. The #JebNoFilter hashtag was introduced on the campaign's official channel but a post on July 17, 2015, had the reverse effect for the campaign's goal of crafting a more relatable Bush. Donning a hoodie made by Thumbtack, a hip brand that features artist designs, Bush gave a nod to the company in an uploaded video filmed in Las Vegas. He pulled the sweatshirt awkwardly over his head and looked into the camera to exclaim: "Eat your heart out, Zuckerberg!" The problem? The sweatshirt was a zip-up, not a pullover, and YouTube users roasted the candidate in the comments section. The no filter video did more to demonstrate an out-of-touch candidate than one that was relatable to young voters. It also became fodder for satire. The feedback loops of social media introduce an element of spontaneity that makes it impossible for campaigns to entirely control the narrative of campaigns and the actions of candidates.

Even light-hearted interactivity online holds risk. Does anyone remember Boaty McBoatface – the name given to a British autonomous underwater vehicle via online poll? Well, when Hillary Clinton used an online poll to select her campaign jam, voters selected a Celine Dion song (Gulati, 2009). The problem? Dion is Canadian – not American – and that made Clinton susceptible to backlash. In 2020 President Trump took to Twitter to congratulate Super Bowl winners, the Kansas City Chiefs, congratulating the "Great State of Kansas." The problem? The franchise is based in Kansas City, *Missouri*. The online ridicule illustrated a president who lacked basic knowledge of U.S. geography. More recently, Florida Governor Ron DeSantis' official presidential campaign announcement was derailed by the technology itself. Twitter servers reportedly could not handle the number of users logged in to Twitter Spaces, its live audio tool, where DeSantis was slated to have a conversation with Elon Musk and officially introduce himself as a 2024 presidential candidate. The conversation launched, albeit with spotty audio and a 30-minute delay. Mainstream news coverage of his announcement focused on the "glitchy" rollout rather than the candidate and the tech snafu dominated headlines across national news outlets including *Politico*, *CNN*, *The New York Times*, *The Wall Street Journal*, and *Fox News*.

Risk may also keep some candidates off certain platforms altogether. With elected officials sounding the alarm over Chinese-owned TikTok, stoking fears of spying, data collection, and misinformation, there seems to be an unease with using the platform for campaign purposes. The gains may not outweigh the risk given that TikTok's users are far younger than the average voter and include many that aren't yet of voting age. Some stoking fears of the platform would likely be called out for campaigning on it; Marco Rubio is just one example of a politician swiftly deleting their TikTok account (Kambhampaty, 2022). Nonetheless, no candidate wants to be absent from a popular digital platform and as technologies reach critical mass, presence becomes a campaign imperative.

Summary

Folding digital-media strategies into electoral campaigns exploded after President Obama's two terms, particularly as he capitalized on Facebook-like functions for his 2008 campaign and explored crafty ways to communicate policy on digital spaces. Candidates continue to grapple with opportune ways to advance their campaigns through digital and social media. And these trends are not unique to presidential politics. Pew (2021) reported that from fall 2016 to fall 2020, social media activity from members of U.S. Congress exploded, with a 586% increase in likes and favorites, a 268% increase in shares and retweets, and a 53% increase in the sheer volume of posts. From Instagram stories to TikTok campaigning, we now see digital strategies deployed even in state and local campaigns.

We should expect to see the strategic use of digital and social media expand but not necessarily in ways and tools we saw in 2008, 2016, or even 2020. Facebook use has plateaued, and Twitter's influence has been at a crossroads since tech giant Elon Musk purchased the platform in 2022. Evolving media habits – such as the public fascination with TikTok and ChatGPT – will continue to shape digital campaign strategies. Emerging tools will continue to provide critical new avenues for candidates to reach voters. We won't always be able to predict which digital tools will be front and center in a given election year, but the one thing that is certain is change, and campaigns willing to embrace the technology of the now will have the advantage in reaching inattentive voters.

Resources and references

Anderson, M. (2015). *More Americans are using social media to connect with politicians.* Pew Research Center. www.pewresearch.org/fact-tank/2015/05/19/more-americans-are-using-social-media-to-connect-with-politicians/

Boukes, M. (2019). Social network sites and acquiring current affairs knowledge: The impact of Twitter and Facebook usage on learning about the news. *Journal of Information Technology & Politics, 16*(1), 36–51.

Brigham, K. (2020, October 17). Trump and Biden are using campaign apps to gather mounds of voter data. *CNBC.* www.cnbc.com/2020/10/17/trump-and-biden-are-using-campaign-apps-to-gather-mounds-of-voter-data.html

Bush, J. [Jeb Bush]. (2015, July 17). *Hoodie: Jeb Bush* [Video]. YouTube. www.youtube.com/watch?v=jBg6hU5zXDA

Collins, T. (2018, January 20). Trump's itchy Twitter thumbs have redefined politics. *CNET.* www.cnet.com/news/politics/donald-trump-twitter-redefines-presidency-politics/

D'Anastasio, C. (2020, October 20). Alexandria Ocasio-Cortez storms Twitch. *Wired.* www.wired.com/story/aoc-among-us-twitch-stream/

Davies, H. (2015, December 11). Ted Cruz using firm that harvested data on millions of unwitting Facebook users. *The Guardian.* www.theguardian.com/us-news/2015/dec/11/senator-ted-cruz-president-campaign-facebook-user-data

Dutta, S., & Fraser, M. (2008, November 18). Barack Obama and the Facebook election. *U.S. News & World Report.* www.usnews.com/opinion/articles/2008/11/19/barack-obama-and-the-facebook-election

Eilperin, J. (2015, May 26). Here's how the first president of the social media age has chosen to connect with Americans. *The Washington Post.* www.washingtonpost.com/news/politics/wp/2015/05/26/heres-how-the-first-president-of-the-social-media-age-has-chosen-to-connect-with-americans/

Feezell, J. T., & Ortiz, B. (2021). "I saw it on Facebook": An experimental analysis of political learning through social media. *Information, Communication & Society, 24*(9), 1283–1302.

Frank, A. (2020, October 22). AOC met more than 400,000 young potential voters on their own turf: Twitch. *Vox.* www.vox.com/2020/10/22/21526625/aoc-twitch-stream-among-us-most-popular-twitch-streams-ever

Gorman, L., & Miller, N. (2022, October 31). *Not just dance videos: How candidates are using TikTok in the U.S. midterms.* The Alliance for Securing Democracy: German Marshall Fund. https://securingdemocracy.gmfus.org/candidates-tiktok-us-midterm-elections-2022/

Gorman, S. (2008, October 17). Obama buys first video game campaign ads. *Reuters.* www.reuters.com/article/us-usa-politics-videogames/obama-buys-first-video-game-campaign-ads-idUSTRE49EAGL20081017

Green, G. [GloZell Green]. (2015, January 23). *GloZell's interview with President Obama* [Video]. YouTube. www.youtube.com/watch?v=nQe7o_Gea-4

Grim, R. (2023, April 14). Marianne Williamson, fusing Bernie Sanders and (early) Jordan Peterson, is taking over TikTok. *The Intercept.* https://theintercept.com/2023/04/14/marianne-williamson-tiktok/

Gulati, J. (2009). The new media environment and the 2008 election. In L. J. Sabato (Ed.), *The year of Obama: How Obama won the White House* (pp. 191–208). Pearson.

Havenstein, H. (2008, November 10). My.BarackObama.com stays online after election. *Computer World.* www.computerworld.com/article/2534052/my-barackobama-com-social-network-stays-online-after-election.html

Jarvey, N. (2015, February 13). How Buzzfeed turned 10 minutes with President Obama into a viral sensation. *The Hollywood Reporter.* www.hollywoodreporter.com/business/digital/how-buzzfeed-turned-10-minutes-773416/

Jennings, R. (2019, December 20). Why selfie lines are crucial to Elizabeth Warren's campaign. *Vox.* www.vox.com/the-goods/2019/9/19/20872718/elizabeth-warren-2020-selfie-line

Kambhampaty, A. P. (2022, March 19). Securing the TikTok vote. *The New York Times.* www.nytimes.com/2022/03/19/style/tiktok-political-campaigns-midterm-elections.html

Lorenz, T. (2020, February 13). Michael Bloomberg's campaign suddenly drops memes everywhere. *The New York Times.* www.nytimes.com/2020/02/13/style/michael-bloomberg-memes-jerry-media.html

Manthey, G. (2020, October 29). Presidential campaigns set new record for social media ad spending. *ABC7.* https://abc7.com/presidential-race-campaign-spending-trump-political-ads-biden/7452228/

Nelson, R. (2018, May 15). Meet the members of Congress who play video games. *Politico Magazine.* www.politico.com/magazine/story/2018/05/15/congress-video-games-scott-peters-darrell-issa-jared-polis-218367/

Park, J., & Smith, D. (2022, November 11). How two corgis and a Pikachu suit helped Kenneth Mejia make history in L.A. controller race. *Los Angeles Times.* www.latimes.com/california/story/2022-11-11/kenneth-mejia-city-controller-race-first-asian-american-la-citywide-office

Petrova, M., Sen, A., & Yildirim, P. (2021). Social media and political contributions: The impact of new technology on political competition. *Management Science, 67*(5), 2997–3021.

Pew. (2013, March 17). *The media and campaign 2012.* Pew Research Center. www.pewresearch.org/journalism/2013/03/17/the-media-and-campaign-2012/

Pew. (2021, September 30). *Charting Congress on social media in the 2016 and 2020 elections.* Pew Research Center. www.pewresearch.org/politics/2021/09/30/charting-congress-on-social-media-in-the-2016-and-2020-elections/

Quah, N. (2020, October 27). The rise of the politician podcast. *Vulture.* www.vulture.com/2020/10/rise-of-the-politician-podcast.html

Robertson, D. (2022, August 19). Wow, politicians are really bad at podcasting. *Politico Magazine.* www.politico.com/news/magazine/2022/08/19/boring-podcasts-00052659

Smith, A. (2009, April 15). *The internet's role in campaign 2008.* Pew Research Center. www.pewresearch.org/internet/2009/04/15/the-internets-role-in-campaign-2008/

Smith, A. (2014, November 3). *Cell phones, social media, and campaign 2014.* Pew Research Center. www.pewresearch.org/internet/2014/11/03/cell-phones-social-media-and-campaign-2014/

Smith, N. (2020, October 22). The gamer voter: Democrats lean into video games to aid Biden campaign. *The Washington Post.* www.washingtonpost.com/video-games/2020/10/22/video-games-2020-presidential-election-biden-trump/

Weinberg, B., & Williams, C. (2006). The 2004 US presidential campaign: Impact of hybrid offline and online "meetup" communities. *Journal of Direct, Data and Digital Marketing, 8*(1), 46–57.

Wired Staff. (2004, January 1). How the internet invented Howard Dean. *Wired.* www.wired.com/2004/01/dean/

Wortham, J. (2012, October 8). The presidential campaign on social media. *The New York Times.* https://archive.nytimes.com/www.nytimes.com/interactive/2012/10/08/technology/campaign-social-media.html?_r=0

7 Trivialization or accessibility? The democratic implications of entertaining the electorate

Oscar Wilde wrote that "life imitates art far more than art imitates life" in his 1889 essay titled *The Decay of Lying*. In today's media environment that so seamlessly integrates entertainment and reality, it is becoming increasingly difficult to test the validity of Wilde's assertion. Media scholar Neil Postman (1985) famously critiqued the television for providing constant amusement, for blurring information with entertainment, and news with spectacle. Today's options for amusement afforded by cable bundles, websites, podcasts, social media, streaming services, games, and artificial intelligence, might be considered Postman's characterization on steroids.

The melding of news and entertainment also means that people see little distinction between news and entertainment. For example, Tina Fey's *Saturday Night Live* impression of vice-presidential candidate Sarah Palin was so spot-on that the public confused quotes from Fey for words spoken by Palin. Fact-checking resource Snopes and news outlets had to clarify that the infamous quote "And I can see Russia from my house" did not belong to Palin but, rather, was a part of Fey's *SNL* script (O'Carroll, 2011). In the long tail, entertainment media attracts more eyes than news and audiences are increasingly skeptical of mainstream news. Consequently, news becomes an entertaining spectacle and fictional programming tackles more serious political issues. According to media scholar Doris Graber (2012, p. 65), entertainment can "serve as alternative sources for understanding the political world." Thus, entertainment media are routinely bridging political realities with fictional worlds. ABC's *The West Wing* brilliantly underscored the intertwined nature of political reality and political entertainment.

The West Wing aired on network television for seven seasons, centering on a cast of characters from the White House's communications staff, including the press secretary, speech writers, pollsters, and the president's chief of staff. The drama's primary purpose was to entertain, but the program also made politics accessible by highlighting governmental processes and providing context to real-world events in a format that reduced barriers for low-information audiences. *The West Wing* primed viewers to empathize with the show's fictional president, and exposure to the show improved viewers' favorability of real-life

DOI: 10.4324/9781003364832-7

presidents Clinton and G. W. Bush (Holbert et al., 2003). In other words, the show humanized the executive branch and real-life presidents by conditioning its audience to evaluate real life presidents through the traits and attributes conveyed by the show's fictional president. Television critics applauded *The West Wing* for its teachable moments, which included a 9/11 episode, a live fictional debate between actors Jimmy Smits and Alan Alda and a day in the life of a press secretary episode.

More than two decades after the final season of *The West Wing* aired in 2006, audiences could choose from an explosion of politically themed entertainment programs including *House of Cards, Scandal, Veep, Homeland, The Wire, Political Animals, Madam Secretary, The Diplomat, The Newsroom, Alpha House,* and *Succession*. At times, fact-checking research and real-life events even shape fictional plots. Former White House Press Secretary Dee Dee Myers was hired to fact-check aspects of the presidency and political process for *The West Wing*. To prepare for his role as Frank Underwood, Kevin Spacey shadowed U.S. Congressman Kevin McCarthy; some *House of Cards* storylines are reportedly based on McCarthy's life. *The Newsroom*, which portrayed its characters as news professionals attempting to restore public trust in an industry struggling against the tides of market demands and sensationalism, based plots off current events such as the 2010 Deepwater Horizon oil spill and the Tea Party movement soon after they unfolded in real life.

As entertainment media tackled more political themes, the news media and political campaigns were looking to integrate more elements from entertainment media. But that relationship was – and can still be – an uncomfortable one. Some scholars felt that leveraging entertainment media would trivialize elections or delegitimize U.S. democracy.

Showbiz political culture: the good, the bad, and the ugly

The television set may seem rather innocuous in today's online world of media abundance, but for decades, it was symbolic of mass entertainment. The television was highly revered and hotly criticized. The medium, which championed visual communication above all else, shaped pop culture, and increased public yearning for entertainment. Some scholars warned that there would be irrevocable political repercussions from television's dominance.

Postman (1985) argued that the showbiz nature of television culture would dilute political life and accelerate public distraction and disengagement. Interestingly, Postman's arguments came just before the media's long tail. With developments in cable, web, streaming content, and social media, his argument is even more compelling in today's media landscape. Postman's gravest concern was the implications this thirst for amusement would have on democracy; he wasn't alone. Scholar Roderick Hart (1996) believed that passive viewing of politics through the entertainment of television would fool us into thinking we are politically involved, essentially replacing action with spectatorship. And the oversaturation of horse race coverage and polling might falsely signal to viewers that our voices are already accounted for in the political process. Political scientist Robert Putnam was uncomfortable with the relationship between entertainment media and civic life. According to Putnam's (2000) time displacement argument, people devoted so much time to television that it left little hours in the day to be politically or civically active. And with so much competing content from media's long tail, a steady decline in the public's appetite for serious news was underway (Prior, 2007).

The shift to visual mediums would have repercussions for not just news audiences but the news product. As we learned in previous chapters, political news coverage would adopt more entertaining characteristics. The language of sport, horse race coverage, and conflict-driven news would make electoral politics feel more like a game.

The explosion of entertainment also expanded the class of inattentive voters and ushered in an era of public cynicism about politics and democratic institutions. Less exposure to serious political news coverage meant less understanding of policy and how democratic institutions operate. That also means more character-based appeals and the increasing personalization of contemporary campaigns, as candidates grapple with a distracted electorate. Nonetheless, that doesn't mean an entertained electorate can't learn a thing or two about candidates and policy or find the motivation to re-engage.

Did you ever have a method for fooling your parents when it came time to eating a loathed vegetable? For me, it was peas. I would hide them under my plate, enclose them in the hollow shell of an eaten baked potato, or, when feeling especially diabolical, discreetly scrape them onto my sister's plate after she finished at the dinner table. But when peas were mixed in with a more palatable food, mashed potatoes for example, I could stomach them. Think of political news as peas for most Americans and entertainment media as the mashed potatoes. When the electorate consumes media primarily for entertainment, they may find political news that they are incidentally exposed to as more digestible than political news as a stand-alone media diet. Before the distractions of digital media had its grip on audiences, some scholars were bullish on the civic benefits of infotainment. Some research indicates that entertainment media may reduce the cognitive barriers for political learning and facilitate a level of engagement from low information voters that may not have transpired without the melding of entertainment and politics (Baum, 2002). This goes back to the peas and mashed potatoes analogy. The mashed potatoes alone may not offer much nutrition, but the incidental exposure to the peas does.

If not for the melding of entertainment and politics, a sizable percentage of the electorate may not learn about the candidates at all. Media choice results in less exposure to news and those who prefer entertainment are learning less and participating less in elections (Prior, 2007). Today's media landscape makes it easy for people to opt out of political life. This is why entertainment-driven campaigns may not only help candidates access the public but also spur incidental learning and motivate others to participate in politics. By political elites coming to the preferred media of low information voters – the space of sitcoms, satire, social media, streaming sites, and influencer accounts – we could see renewed political engagement.

Although it's difficult to discern the long-term effects of entertainment-driven campaigns, they have the potential to reinvigorate subgroups of voters. Clinton's 1992 campaigning on late-night television motivated young voters and Black voters to show up to the polls; Obama's emphasis on social media spiked turnout among young voters and first-time voters in 2008; and Trump's Twitter-fueled campaign in 2016 engaged voters in rural and manufacturing reliant states that felt neglected by establishment politicians. And if we look at recent voter turnout figures, campaigns run through entertainment media may drive more people to the polls.

Voter turnout in 2020 topped 62% of voting age Americans (DeSilver, 2022). In fact, data show a slow but steady increase in voter turnout since the 1988 presidential election, after campaigns began to drift away from the confines of traditional news media and waded out to more entertaining platforms to connect with voters. Voter turnout in midterm elections, historically weaker than presidential years, reached a 45-year high in 2018 and increased again in 2022, with approximately 52% of eligible voters casting a ballot (Murphy, 2023). But if campaigns want to build on these trends and keep low information voters engaged, campaigns must continue monitoring the media landscape and evolve strategies to reflect the media diets of the electorate. The turbulent last couple of years across media industries suggest campaigns will have their work cut out for them.

Uncertainties in today's media landscape

Mainstream news companies continue to suffer from a turbulent couple of years. Layoffs at ABC, CNN, *The New York Times*, and *Los Angeles Times* drew considerable news attention. CNN is reeling from the abrupt firing of chief executive Chris Licht, a controversial live Trump's townhall event, and a ratings-squeeze that has the cable network trailing Fox, MSNBC, and even far right Newsmax. *The Washington Post*'s chief executive and publisher Fred Ryan also resigned in 2023, citing frustration over political polarization. Nate Silver took to social media predicting that *FiveThirtyEight*, a prominent source of political information, expects to leave ABC as widespread layoffs affect operations (Albeck-Ripka, 2023). Academics are also sounding the bell on local and regional newspapers folding, resulting in a greater percentage of the electorate living in **news deserts**, defined as geographic areas where people have no or limited access to news and are sparsely covered by news outlets. News deserts may steer even more people toward entertainment and toward less credible sources of information.

Media companies once thought of as success stories of digital age are also facing turmoil. Vice Media (which includes Vice News) filed for Chapter 11 bankruptcy in 2023. Social site Buzzfeed announced not only layoffs in 2023 but also the closure of its news division, which employed veteran journalists and earned the Pulitzer Prize. And streaming companies and social media are also looking ahead with looming uncertainty. First, streaming platforms have struggled since recovery from the pandemic. People are traveling, dining out, attending mass events from music festivals to graduations and, consequently, spending less time binge-watching shows. Netflix, Roku, Disney+, Hulu, Spotify, and HBO Max all announced layoffs over the past two years. Streaming platforms have increased subscription prices and cracked down on shared accounts across different households. As television networks and streaming companies tighten their belts, writers have taken to the picket line.

The 2023 writers' strike of hundreds of members of the Writers Guild of America surpassed 60 days by the end of June. In negotiating with the Alliance of Motion Pictures and Television Producers, the writers seek pay increases, policies limiting AI in the writing process, and more equitable streaming residuals, or compensation for when a program is syndicated on streaming platforms. The last writers' strike, which lasted 100 days in 2007, cost the California economy roughly $2 billion. If the 2023 strike spans 90 days, industry analysts predict an economic loss of approximately $3 billion, with the entertainment sector hit hardest (Gerber & White, 2023). With schools reopening post-COVID-19, less of the workforce telecommuting and more people seeking amusements outside the home, upheaval is also afoot in the tech industry. New competition in the social media market and the mainstreaming of artificial intelligence is luring audiences to new digital distractions.

As young people have migrated to other platforms, Facebook rebranded itself to Meta in 2021. As social life resumed normalcy, the hot tech market cooled, prompting layoffs at Facebook, Microsoft, and Google. Elon Musk's acquisition of Twitter in 2022 signaled a period of extensive layoffs and nervous advertisers. Some users, disgruntled over new ownership and policies, threatened to migrate to social networking alternative Mastodon. And although the popularity of TikTok and ChatGPT isn't in question, the social consequences of them remain debated. Some political elites and thought leaders praise the technologies; others are horrified by how they may be manipulated. Even entertainment media, with films like *M3GAN* (2023), are grappling with the societal fears and ethics of artificial intelligence.

Although an AI-designed doll is unlikely to unleash violent havoc in upcoming election cycles, there is growing trepidation over the capabilities of AI enabling media industries to replace writers and journalists, ultimately threatening the authenticity of creative works and newsgathering. Spotify recently started to police and remove AI-generated music from its platform. In June 2023, President Biden traveled to Silicon Valley to meet with tech experts over mounting concerns over the capabilities of AI, reflecting an uneasy relationship between federal regulators and emerging media technology.

The melding of entertainment and electoral politics evolved from significant changes in the media consumption habits of the electorate. The latest shakeout in the media landscape will most assuredly have implications for the direction of political campaign communication.

Future directions for political campaign communication

As campaigns navigate entertainment media, candidates will continue seeking cameos on sitcoms, dramas, and devote time to the soft news format to connect with voters. As cable companies experience **cord cutting**, meaning a loss in subscribers to streaming platforms, we should see more of this engagement on programs offered by streaming platforms than traditional network television. We could see candidates launch continuous streams providing voyeuristic access to their job functions or campaigns, or see them launch their own channels, a move that Trump has pondered publicly as the relationship between he and Fox News has strained.

Could we even be one or two election cycles away from presidential primary fantasy sports leagues? Perhaps it's not so far-fetched given the prevalence of sports rhetoric and game frames in contemporary politics. After all, there are now online fantasy leagues for *The Bachelor*. Election coverage and the way voters engage could eventually mirror a reality television competition. And as political coverage feels more like competitive sport, gaming platforms are emerging as a shiny new campaign toy.

As candidates embed ads in video games, we could see strategies expand to include virtual campaign stumps. Like the way rapper Travis Scott performed a ten-minute concert within *Fortnite*, candidates could hold virtual rallies and speeches within games or footage from debates and other campaign events could surface in popular game franchises. And now that some politicians are becoming gamers, gamers can soon be politicians. A *Sims*-like game expected to drop in advance of the 2024 election will allow users to role play life in public office by creating their own politician the way sports games let users build athlete avatars with varying strengths and weaknesses. *Political Arena*, a project with campaign strategists on the payroll as consultants, lets users deploy strategy, legislate, and allocate resources for their politician (Summers, 2021).

Celebrities should continue to interject themselves in campaigns, as they seek elected office or visibly align themselves with candidates by raising funds and releasing video endorsements to their following. As the definition of celebrity has expanded in the era of reality television and social media, influencers with niche audiences should be sought out even more in coming elections. Just as media audiences have become fragmented, the electorate is fragmented in who they idolize and follow. Perhaps we even see paid partnerships through platforms like Cameo normalized or outsider celebrities appointed to cabinet positions or named as running mates.

As some candidates have found a footing in podcasting, Twitter Spaces, which hosts live audio conversations, could become a useful tool for campaigns and Musk hopes to offer payment features (which may be leveraged for campaign fundraising). But Musk will have competition. In July 2023, Meta unveiled its latest social media platform, Threads, which will create a competing digital public sphere where celebrities, thought leaders, and political elites are expected to intermingle on an app-based platform with a design that resembles a striking similarity to Twitter. But some politicians may simply prefer image-based platforms to gain notice and generate headlines. Showing skin, through shirtless social media images and workout videos, is one way fringe candidate Robert F. Kennedy, Jr. is forcing an inattentive public and gawking news media to take notice of his Instagram account. Nonetheless, video is where the social media market is at.

Companies have prioritized video to stay competitive in a market that seems poised for TikTok dominance. One thing that remains certain of young voters: their preference for video communication and their preference for temporary content. Therefore, we could see an explosion of digital shorts that can accommodate platforms like TikTok, Snapchat, and Instagram stories that enable fleeting and seemingly authentic forms of communication. And political scientists are opining about the role artificial intelligence could play in political campaigns.

AI could help campaigns narrowly target and personalize communication or spread misinformation. The Republican National Committee used AI in 2023 as a counter to Biden's official launch of his reelection campaign. AI was deployed to create apocalyptic imagery suggestive of a bleak future with Biden reelected. ChatGPT is creating a stir in almost all aspects of civic life, including political campaigns. Florida Governor Ron DeSantis, a 2024 Republican candidate for president, reportedly used AI to generate deepfake images of Donald Trump cozily embracing Dr. Anthony Fauci (Nehamas, 2023), and media critics have suggested the candidate's memoir could be coauthored by ChatGPT.

Artificial intelligence could quite likely emerge as a time and personnel-saving method for churning out campaign speeches and talking points, a resource for strategy, and a research tool for learning about communities and geographic regions along the campaign trail. AI could also be weaponized as a tool for ideological indoctrination. Conservatives have accused ChatGPT of having a liberal "woke" bias and some elites have pushed for right wing versions (Saska, 2023). Tools such as AI, Cameo, and even meme and influencer strategies are unlikely to have candidates draw much attention to them publicly, but if these platforms are used effectively and ultimately normalized, they will become campaign imperatives just as soft news, political cameos, and celebrity endorsements have.

Summary

What we know about media consumption habits of the electorate in the era of media abundance is that candidates no longer can bypass these once seen as trivializing platforms. The critics underestimated the power and appeal of entertainment media and political communication scholars have often overlooked that campaigns are being run almost entirely through entertainment media. Today, candidates must devote more resources, time, and campaign strategy to entertaining platforms, often leveraging these platforms more frequently than – and often in place of – news and information media.

Ultimately, the argument this text delivers is not that these trends are inherently beneficial or problematic to democracy but, rather, are non-negotiable for campaigns, now deeply embedded within electoral strategy, and are quite directly dictated by the evolving media consumption habits of the U.S. electorate and audience fragmentation. To reach the masses, especially those inattentive to politics, campaigns have learned to prioritize engagement with entertainment media. To emphasize news and traditional avenues of campaign communication over entertainment would be a miscalculation in the era of media abundance. Campaigns must continue to adapt and embrace new platforms and trends regardless of how uncomfortable they may first seem for candidates and strategists. To connect with an electorate that continues to seek amusement, campaigns must carefully monitor the consumption habits of the audiences they seek to persuade. Doing so will not guarantee electoral success but will give candidates a fighting chance in the distracting environment known as media's long tail.

Resources and references

Albeck-Ripka, L. (2023, April 25). Nate Silver, FiveThirtyEight founder, expects to depart ABC amid layoffs. *The New York Times.* www.nytimes.com/2023/04/25/business/media/nate-silver-abc-disney-fivethirtyeight.html

Baum, M. A. (2002). Sex, lies, and war: How soft news brings foreign policy to the inattentive public. *American Political Science Review, 96*(1), 91–109.

DeSilver, D. (2022, November 1). *Turnout in the U.S. has soared in recent elections but by some measures still trails that of many other countries.* Pew Research Center. www.pewresearch.org/fact-tank/2022/11/01/turnout-in-u-s-has-soared-in-recent-elections-but-by-some-measures-still-trails-that-of-many-other-countries/

Gerber, M., & White, R. D. (2023, May 8). How much will the writers' strike cost L.A.? Much more than the 2007 stoppage, experts say. *Los Angeles Times.* www.latimes.com/business/story/2023-05-08/economic-fallout-writers-strike-losses-2007-stoppage

Graber, D. A. (2012). *On media: Making sense of politics.* Oxford University Press.

Hart, R. P. (1996). Easy citizenship: Television's curious legacy. *Annals of the American Academy of Political and Social Science, 546,* 109–119.

Holbert, R. L., Pillion, O., Tschida, D. A., Armfield, G. G., Kinder, K., Cherry, K. L., & Daulton, A. R. (2003). The West Wing as endorsement of the U.S. presidency:

Expanding the bounds of priming in political communication. *Journal of Communication, 53*(3), 427–443.

Murphy, J. (2023, May 3). Midterm turnout stayed high in 2022: These states topped the list. *NBC News.* https://broncoathletics.com/news/2023/6/12/womens-track-and-field-ayana-fields-named-ccaa-female-athlete-of-the-year.aspx

Nehamas, N. (2023, June 8). DeSantis campaign uses apparently fake images to attack Trump on Twitter. *The New York Times.* www.nytimes.com/2023/06/08/us/politics/desantis-deepfakes-trump-fauci.html

O'Carroll, E. (2011, June 3). Political misquotes: The 10 most famous things never actually said. *The Christian Science Monitor.* www.csmonitor.com/USA/Politics/2011/0603/Political-misquotes-The-10-most-famous-things-never-actually-said/I-can-see-Russia-from-my-house!-Sarah-Palin

Postman, N. (1985). *Amusing ourselves to death: Public discourse in the age of show business.* Penguin.

Prior, M. (2007). *Post-broadcast democracy: How media choice increase inequality in political involvement and polarizes elections.* Cambridge University Press.

Putnam, R. D. (2000). *Bowling alone: The collapse and revival of American community.* Simon & Schuster.

Saska, J. (2023, May 25). AI could swing the 2024 elections, campaign pros say – but not like you think. *Roll Call.* https://rollcall.com/2023/05/25/ai-could-sway-the-2024-elections-campaign-pros-say-but-not-like-you-think/

Summers, J. (2021, November 4). In this case, politics is a (video) game: "All things considered". *NPR.* www.npr.org/2021/11/04/1051381706/in-this-case-politics-is-a-video-game

Index